Designing Buildings That Work

The McGraw-Hill Designing with Systems Series

ERIC TEICHOLZ, *Consulting Editor*

Stitt   Systems Drafting (1980)

Daryanani   Building Systems Design with Programmable Calculators (1980)

Stitt   Systems Graphics: Breakthroughs in Drawing Production and Project Management for Architects, Designers, and Engineers (1983)

Teicholz   CAD/CAM Handbook (1985)

Stitt   Designing Buildings That Work: The Architect's Problem Prevention Sourcebook (1985)

Teicholz   CIM Handbook (1987)

Gerlach   A/E Transition to CADD (1987)

Designing Buildings That Work

The Architect's Problem Prevention Sourcebook

Fred A. Stitt

McGRAW-HILL BOOK COMPANY
New York   St. Louis   San Francisco   Auckland
Bogotá   Hamburg   Johannesburg   London   Madrid
Mexico   Montreal   New Delhi   Panama   Paris
São Paulo   Singapore   Sydney   Tokyo   Toronto

Library of Congress Cataloging in Publication Data
Stitt, Fred A.
   Designing buildings that work.

   (The McGraw-Hill designing with systems series)
   1. Architectural design—Handbooks, manuals, etc.
I. Title.   II. Series.
NA2750.S74   1985   729   84-23398
ISBN 0-07-047952-6

1234567890   DOC/DOC   898765

ISBN 0-07-047952-6

The editors for this book were Joan Zseleczky and Barbara B.
Toniolo, the design supervisor was Mark E. Safran, and the pro-
duction supervisor was Thomas G. Kowalczyk. It was set in
Melior by University Graphics, Inc.

Printed and bound by R. R. Donnelley & Sons Company

To my first mentor in architecture,
HOWARD ROARK

Contents

Preface

This book tells how to design buildings in the most efficient and effective way possible. Step by step, it explains the following:

1. How to pre-establish the limits and options regarding a new building's size, shape, structure, environmental systems, construction, and materials. Those decisions can and should be made before starting any design sketching. If such decisions aren't established in advance, chances are the original designs will be based on inadequate information and false assumptions and will have to be scrapped.

2. How to gather data from the client and building users to establish an objective basis for creating and judging the building plans that follow.

3. How to use systematic design procedures to create the best possible building plans in the least amount of time.

4. How to use spatial and structural rules of thumb to establish reasonable design assumptions when precise figures are not available.

5. How to apply systematic problem-solving methods used by other professionals to the problems of building design.

6. How to avoid the most common errors in building-to-site relationship, mechanical design, lighting, acoustics, and construction coordination.

7. How to use a design checklist to record, coordinate, and track the multitude of decisions that are made and often remade several times over throughout a building design project.

8. How to build a facilities management data base from all the information created during the design and documentation process. This turns the information in your drawings and specifications into a permanent asset which can be used to attract future clients, to guide your design and production staff in future projects, and to provide continuing consulting service to your past design clients long after the original buildings are completed.

The steps and techniques described here have been collected through nearly twenty years of observation of effective and ineffective design processes in architectural offices all across the country. They're good data. They work.

The information included here is as valid and useful for designing small buildings as large ones. It works well for interior design and space planning and has many applications in long-range master planning. It's suitable for the student and beginner as well as the experienced design professional. I know that such universal usefulness is sometimes falsely advertised to prod book sales, but it's all true in this case.

The reader is assumed either to have a reasonable background knowledge of design office procedures and construction methods or to be in the process of acquiring that knowledge. The information here is also quite helpful to building owners, design clients, and facilities managers.

FRED A. STITT

What Is "High-Speed Design"?

"A design is what the designer has when time and money have run out."

—Murphy

What do designers and planners actually do when they design something?

Traditionally, a designer will review the characteristics of a design problem. He or she will think on it for a while and sketch some ideas. That's followed by more layers of sketching to test and revise the ideas until they work out to a reasonably satisfactory overall solution.

The process often gets off to a rapid start because of the excitement of dealing with a new problem. Then it bogs down as the first impetuous solutions which handle parts of the problem turn out not to handle all the problem. Or the process may be slowed from the outset while awaiting the arrival of a mysterious component called "inspiration." It gets even slower when the long-sought inspiration proves to be half-baked and has to be tossed out entirely.

The process can be observed in one or another of the various aforementioned stages any day in almost any design office in the country.

1

There's another kind of design process—the subject of this book. It might be called "design management," but that phrase is a little ponderous at this point. To dramatize its operational essence, let's call it "high-speed design."

Over the years some designers and planners have invented remarkably effective techniques for gathering data about a design problem and for organizing that information in a way that leads the problem toward "solving itself."

Designers have discovered diverse, faster, and more effective ways of analyzing design information, assimilating it, and, finally, expressing it in a comprehensive creative synthesis. I have spent over 20 years observing and recording these techniques. The techniques allow any designer or planner to plan his or her work so that it can then be done with a maximum of certainty and speed. Many such techniques are strictly personal and work only for a few individuals; others have a universal logic and work for virtually anyone who applies them. The best tools of both types, the best of the best, are laid out for you in this book.

The most important tool in this book is in Appendix B. It's the Predesign and Planning Checklist. You can put that part of the book to work immediately with or without the other information in these chapters. Appendix A explains how to use the checklist. Feel free to review the explanatory material in Appendix A before working with other parts of this book; however, it will help you considerably to read Chapter 1 first.

This book covers the how-to essentials of "speed design," mainly predesign, programming, planning methodology, planning rules of thumb, and systematic problem solving. A later volume will emphasize more technical details and reference data on energy analysis, feasibility studies, life-cycle costing, and other useful concepts.

Meanwhile, if you're interested in sources of data on high-speed design and problem-solving methodology that have appeared since this book was published, send a self-addressed, stamped envelope (1 ounce postage) to Fred Stitt, *Guidelines*, Box 456, Orinda, California 94563.

chapter 1

Predesign and Programming— The First Steps

"You can't be lost as long as you don't know where you're supposed to be."

—Murphy

THE STEPS OF "PREDESIGN"

"Predesign" means making all the design decisions that can be made before starting on schematic design drawings. The client, for example, usually knows roughly the number and kinds of rooms the building will require. The architect will know the zoning and code restrictions that will limit building height and class of construction. And the architect and client may agree, for reasons of construction speed and economy, on a very specific structural and construction system. That combined information will tell the designer a great deal about what the building will be like before pencil touches paper (or long before the first lines are generated on the video display).

Designers run into trouble when there are too few predesign

data. The client may know the general disposition of rooms, for example, but won't necessarily know their best relationships. The designer who fails to preestablish the best room relationships with the client, according to objective standards, can spend weeks arbitrarily arranging and rearranging rooms in a plan until something more or less works out. And it still may not be settled.

After the designer's lengthy work, the client or design partners may set the whole process back a few more weeks by insisting on new plan studies in pursuit of a "better" solution. Those changes, even good ones, invariably have a negative effect on other aspects of the plan. Moving a storeroom may restrict a neighboring space, which may mean shifting a corridor, which affects the building core, and on and on.

Every new change leads to more arranging and rearranging, until time and money run out and the project *has* to move into the next phase. (Then, often enough, plan changes continue right through working drawings, at enormous cost.)

Clients know a great deal about what they will require in their building, but they often have to wait for design drawings or models or even working drawings before they have a chance to say: "No, that won't work for us. *This* is what we have to have."

When clients don't fully know what will work best for them, you have two choices of how to find out:

1. You can go ahead and design and draw or build models of what you think will work best, or
2. You can find out the primary criteria the client uses—what's most important in making design choices in general—and then verbally review choices before building them into design documents.

This chapter tells how to clearly identify major design decisions with the client before starting schematic drawings. The data you gather by following the fact-finding checklist in this chapter will give you the best possible base of information for starting on design. The fact-finding data are organized in a way that makes everything that follows far less subject to misinterpretation, error, backtracking, and revision than traditional methods of informal predesign data gathering.

Once you identify the essential attributes of the overall building, you can proceed to detailed interior spatial planning, as described in the next chapter. That process may very well lead to modifications of decisions made in the first phase. Once you've confirmed overall general decisions, you can zero in with increasingly more specific decisions on site work, structure, interior and exterior construction systems, materials, and building products. Later, you'll get even more precise as you decide details of finishes and appurtenances.

After you get beyond identifying the controlling general conditions of the project and developing your preliminary building plan, you can switch to the much more detailed predesign and planning checklist that's laid out in Appendix B. Use this checklist at every design decision session to document everything that happens during the job and why it happens. This checklist approach can save you a fortune in time savings and error prevention on even just one job.

IDENTIFYING THE MAJOR ATTRIBUTES OF THE PROJECT

The goal is to create an abstract model of the completed building that incorporates all the information that exists or can be developed prior to starting any drawings.

There is a hierarchy, a sequence of dependency in any chain of decisions made about a building. To illustrate the point, here is the sequence of data and decisions required for a typical building project—starting from the end and moving to the beginning:

1. One of the final decisions of a designer is finishes. Finishes are limited by the choices of materials.

2. Choices of materials are limited by the construction methods, framing, and structure.

3. Construction, framing, and structure are limited by circumstances of budget, required construction speed, building shape, heights, and spans of the building.

4. The building shape, heights, and spans that most affect structure are restricted by site and zoning limitations and are finally determined by interior space sizes, shapes, and relationships.

5. Choices of spatial sizes and relationships are limited by the building's population, circulation system, and equipment.

6. Building population, circulation system, and equipment are determined by the building's primary and secondary functions.

7. The building's functions are decided by the client's overall values, needs, and plans as qualified by financial, regulatory, siting, and other circumstantial restraints.

At each step of the way there are a multitude of choices, but the number of choices is limited by the restraints established by previous choices. Thus, the value and purpose of predesign are that it gives the designer a workable set of limits.

Here is an abbreviated start-to-finish sequence of design decisions similar to that used by several large architectural and interior design firms:

Overall size and shape, determined by function and occupancy and by external restrictions

Site planning to accommodate the building functions and the building shell

Space planning

Structure

Interior materials and finishes

Exterior materials and finishes

This first phase of predesign creates an abstract design of the building as a whole in words and numbers. Later predesign decision-making sessions will cycle downward in smaller and smaller units—from the building as a whole, to subdivisions, to individual rooms, to individual elements and features of each room. These smaller divisions are described in the chapters that follow.

The Preliminary Design Program Checklist

Identifying the Major Attributes of the Project

Here is the basic attribute identification process in a checklist format:

_____ Client:

_____ Client representatives (names, titles, addresses, phone numbers):

_____ Chain of responsibility or decision making in client's organization:

_____ Source of financing:

_____ Client's general stated needs and desires:

_____ Overriding goal or purpose of building project:

_____ Primary building functions:

VERY IMPORTANT: MAKE SEPARATE LISTS OF SUBFUNCTIONS, SITE FEATURES, AND ROOMS AND SPACES, AND REVIEW THOSE SPACE NEEDS WITH THE USER QUESTIONNAIRE SHOWN AT THE END OF THIS CHAPTER.

_____ Secondary building functions:

_____ Estimated construction budget:
Phases

_____ Estimated construction deadline(s):
Phases

_____ Estimated occupant population type(s) and size(s) to fulfill stated function(s):

_____ Special equipment to fulfill stated function(s):

_____ Special furnishings to fulfill stated function(s):

_____ Building or building division size(s) to accommodate population, circulation, furnishings, and equipment:

_____ Future building functions and populations:

USE SEPARATE SHEET TO LIST OR RECORD SUBFUNCTIONS AND LISTS OF ROOMS OR SPATIAL FUNCTIONS.

_____ Limits or allowable size of future expansion:

_____ Existing facilities to be part of this project:

_____ Existing facilities to use as design or planning examples for this project:

To make preliminary height and shaping decisions that affect spatial allocation, external and internal, determine the following.

External Restraints on Building Area, Shape, and Height

_____ Total lot dimensions and area:

_____ Usable lot area:

_____ Setback restrictions:

_____ Other zoning restrictions:

_____ Deed covenants:

_____ Easements:

_____ Rights-of-way:

_____ Air rights:

_____ Facade easement:

_____ Existing construction:

_____ Solar orientation:

_____ Building shadow restrictions:

_____ Required public spaces:

_____ Other:

Internal Restraints on Building Area, Shape, and Height

_____ Groupings of population or function that require large open spaces:

_____ Groupings of population or function that require courts or atria:

_____ Groupings of population or function that require direct access to exterior ground level:

_____ Functions that require high-ceiling interior spaces:

_____ Functions requiring daylight:

_____ Views:

_____ Other:

Figure 1.1　Basic predesign decision making can most conveniently be done manually with a checklist. But all such data then have to be input to a computer as part of documenting every step of a design project. (Courtesy of Herman Miller.)

USER QUESTIONNAIRE

This questionnaire is to establish user desires and needs on a room by room basis and to identify important relationships between rooms. Copy this form or your own version of it in quantity and be sure every interior and exterior space has been recorded.

PROJECT _____   SPACE NAME _____

FLOOR OR LEVEL_____   DEPARTMENT_____

SPACE SIZE _____   SPACE AREA _____   HEIGHT_____

EXISTING EQUIVALENT ROOM NAME, NUMBER, SIZE, AREA, AND HEIGHT:

_____

TITLE OF USER(S) _____

NAME OR ID CODE _____

OTHER SPACES THAT RELATE TO THIS SPACE AND NOTE RANKING OF IMPORTANCE OF RELATIONSHIP TO THIS SPACE:
Mandatory--4   Important--3   Desirable--1   Undesirable--X

_____   _____

_____   _____

_____   _____

_____   _____

_____   _____

FURNITURE:
(List by quantity, type, size, and code. Attach separate list for complex room types.)

_____

_____

_____

_____

SCHEMATIC FURNITURE PLAN:
(Note by type and no. Use bottom of second page for complex room types.)

11

USER QUESTIONNAIRE   (cont.)

EQUIPMENT:
(List by quantity, size, and no.)

_____

_____

_____

_____

NUMBER OF PEOPLE:
(List by type/titles.)

_____

_____

_____

_____

_____

ARCHITECTURAL FINISHES:
(Use code or abbreviations.)

FLOOR _____   WALLS _____

BASE _____   WAINSCOT _____

SPECIAL WALL _____   GLAZED WALL _____

DRAPES/BLINDS _____   CEILING _____

DOOR(S) _____   WINDOW(S) _____

ACOUSTICAL TREATMENT _____

STORAGE _____

CABINET WORK _____

PLUMBING FIXTURES

_____
_____
_____

COMMUNICATIONS

Phone _____
Computer _____
Dictaphone _____
Pneumatic tube _____
Delivery slot/window _____
(Other) _____

HVAC

_____
_____

ELECTRICAL

Outlets _____
Switching _____
Special loads _____

LIGHTING

Ceiling _____
Spot _____
Display _____
Task _____

(Other) _____

13

Just What Is It That Designers and Planners Do?

*"Professional planners and consultants don't
necessarily know more than other people, they're just
better organized and have slides."*

—Murphy

Designers and planners don't just move shapes around or "draw plans." These are among the least and last things they do.

What designers do includes dealing with sometimes capricious and irrational clients who insist you can squeeze 10,000 square feet of function into 5000 square feet of space, or a $500,000 design into a $100,000 budget.

Designers help clients get variances from zoning laws. They help people borrow money to finance a building. They often sit for hours listening to gibberish at the offices of regulatory agencies. They sometimes spend weeks working on design presentations to show to a client who has decided to hire another firm but is embarrassed to say so.

Designers fly around in dangerous airplanes in bad weather to deliver drawings and collect fees. For relaxation they spend weekends sorting through memos, sketches, meeting notes, and letters to figure out who really made the decisions that led to the cost overruns that have now dragged the firm into court.

That's the day-to-day reality of it all.

The day-to-day tasks are supportive, that is, they exist as part of the larger job of designing worthwhile environments for people. And that job encompasses a whole universe of ideas including ethics, politics, aesthetics, psychology, epistemology, and metaphysics.

Designers sometimes aren't much fun to talk to because they are so deeply involved in the world of ideas they would rather listen to pig grunts than endure normal conversational small talk. Ultimately it is the world of ideas that motivates designers. Abstract conceptualization and ideology are what underlie the physical reality of their designs. Anyone who seeks to understand the concrete reality of their constructs without knowing the ideas behind them will miss the point entirely.

Besides the peculiar mix of day-to-day trivia and the compelling internal universe of values and ideas, designers also wrestle with the uncompromising universe of physical reality: the treacherous soil below and relentless weather above. Designers have the awesome chore of making sure that a building's plumbing, ductwork, and structure don't all try to occupy precisely the same cubic area and that roof drainpipes don't show up in the executive conference room. At that personal level, they face the challenge of making sure that people can find their way through a designed environment, can read the signs, won't trip on an unexpected 4-inch drop in floor level, won't catch their sleeves on a handrail when rushing downstairs, and won't die from smoke inhalation or incineration in a fire.

How do designers watch over all these things? Actually many don't, or they don't do it thoroughly. Routine scrutiny of most any building will quickly demonstrate that fact. But many others do. They do it by what we call "method." That is, they've established routines and rules of practice that allow them to sort out vast numbers of specifics through an immense hierarchy of human values, needs, and desires. What makes their work seem almost magical at times is that effective design methods allow them to integrate specifics, values, constraints, and financial and political needs that are often in raging conflict with one another.

The key to method is "planning," but planning in a different sense from what most people think of. It means *real* planning, *preplanning*. That means making the plan of the planning process. It means designing the pattern or process that controls the design. *That's* the level of planning and design that allows someone to encompass all those diverse and often contradictory conditions designers must bring together.

chapter 2

Space Planning

"If you call what you are doing a System, then it can take the blame when things go wrong."

—*Murphy's Prescriptive Alibi*

AN INTRODUCTION TO SYSTEMATIC PLANNING

Most planning of sites and buildings boils down to arranging spaces in a sensible relationship to one another and to the world outside. A good plan does that. A bad one doesn't. Any normal human being can ultimately come up with a good spatial plan for any project. The difference is that a trained designer can do it faster. And a designer trained in systematic planning methods can do it even faster still. And with more reliable results.

The typical designer uses an "intuitive" approach consisting of some data gathering, some logical problem solving, some inspiration, and lots of trial and error. One design partner describes it like this: "You start with obvious relationships, like putting the main entrance toward the street, public rooms near the entrance, service rooms toward the back; other rooms fit in here and there. Then you start zeroing in and discover some problems; you move a couple of rooms around, and then a couple more. Then you discover you forgot some vital consideration, or you get a great new idea, and start over."

Rarely are job requirements so clear and simple that a workable plan can evolve through one or two sketches. Plan conflicts arise; important room relationships are overlooked. You get a good idea for the plan but find, even after trying dozens of spatial rearrangements, that some room grouping within it will not work—which ultimately invalidates the entire scheme.

Why does it get so complicated?

It's the mathematics involved. The rooms in even a small building can be arranged in thousands of possible relationships. The number of possible arrangements of spaces within a building goes like this:

Number of spaces	Possible arrangements
1	1
2	2
3	6
4	24
5	120
6	720
7	5,040
8	40,320
9	362,880
10	3,628,800

That's only 10 spaces. At 20 and 30, the number of possible relationships becomes astronomical. And this doesn't take into account the unlimited possible variations in shaping and proportion, or the introduction of exterior spaces and functions, or considerations of variations in heights. It's a lot to cope with, and that's why it can all get so tangled.

Naturally, program requirements limit the options for acceptable arrangements in a real job, but the possible number of variations remains immense, even in small projects.

One of the limitations of traditional "intuitive" design is that the designer cannot normally carry every pertinent program requirement in his or her head. The best the designer can do is try to remember only the most crucial requirements and—once these are accommodated—check back to see what's been overlooked.

FAST-TRACK DESIGN WITH THE LINK AND NODE DIAGRAM

There is a way to keep all programmed spatial requirements visible so that they cannot be readily overlooked or forgotten. And in the process, you can quickly develop a schematic building plan that resolves spatial or circulation conflicts and reveals where all building spaces should be placed relative to one another. This schematic or outline plan, a systematic version of the old bubble diagram, will save days and weeks of design time over the traditional intuitive, "inspiration plus trial and error" approach.

The method's steps are shown in the following example, which is a simple abstraction concisely conveying the essentials of the system.

1. In this example, a set of five rooms is drawn. Small circles are used to symbolize the rooms. In an actual project, the circles would be identified with room names.

2. Rooms that relate to one another are connected with a line. In this example we assume that room A has a direct functional relationship with room B as, say, when one wishes the kitchen to be next to the dining room in a residence.

3. All relationships are identified in turn with connective lines. This is called a "link and node" diagram.

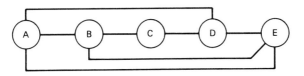

4. A new diagram is drawn in which spaces are relocated to reduce the length of the longest lines. In addition, the symbols are changed in size to represent proportionate sizes of the programmed rooms. At this point the link and node diagram has

been transformed into a bubble diagram—the beginning of a schematic plan.

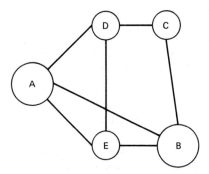

5. The line between A and B that crosses the D–E line reveals a plan conflict. Since each line represents a relationship, a desirable proximity between rooms, the existence of any crossed lines means two rooms are trying to share the same space. Conflict. A new arrangement is created to eliminate the crossed lines and to equalize all connective lines as much as possible.

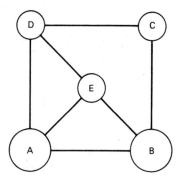

6. The bubbles are pulled together into a tight diagram that incorporates the room proportions and desired spatial relationships.

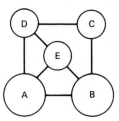

7. The final bubble diagram is transposed into abstract schematic plan options. Any plan that is developed from this basic structure of relationships will meet the criteria established in the original link and node diagram.

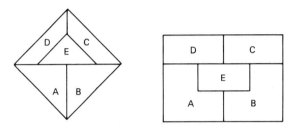

A diagrammatic frame of reference has now been established for planning the building. The preceding diagram meets the original criteria. If plans are created that depart from this frame of reference, they will have built-in conflicts in functional relationships and circulation.

The average designer, doing a similar exercise through trial and error sketching, could easily fill several sheets with doodles before hitting an optimal solution. "Optimal" in this sense means a set of room relationships that meets all stated needs and adds no problems or conflicts in function or circulation.

The reader is encouraged to test this method first on a medium-sized project. In doing so, keep the following points in mind:

- Care is needed to avoid forgetting or misplacing connective lines. Compare each new diagram with the original to make sure all connections are accounted for.

- In step 4, it generally helps to move the bubble with the largest number of connections toward the center of the new diagram.

- In step 5, several attempts may be required to equalize line lengths and eliminate crossed lines. If some lines are extremely difficult or impossible to uncross, an unavoidable plan conflict is indicated. This may be resolved by reconsidering the desirability of the room relationships, splitting room functions among other spaces, or giving some spaces multiple functions.

The next sections of this chapter describe refinements and elaborations that make systematic planning more reliable and effective when doing larger building plans.

THE NEXT FAST-TRACK DESIGN TOOL:
THE SPATIAL ALLOCATION DIAGRAM

We've seen how to quickly diagram room relationships in an orderly fashion. Now how do we determine that order to begin with? Who says which spaces go where? And why? And in case of conflict, which relationships have priority?

Here's one way to determine the order. It's called an "interaction matrix" or "spatial allocation diagram." Here is a partial example of what one looks like:

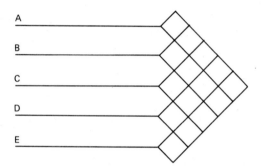

It shows the main features of the chart. Programmed interior and exterior spaces are listed down the left side. Each square in the grid connects two listed spaces and provides a place to record an evaluation of the *importance* of the relationship between each two spaces.

All evaluations of the importance of relationships between spaces are rated and marked on the chart according to this scale:

Close proximity rating	
Mandatory	3
Important	2
Desirable	1
Unimportant	0
Undesirable	X

(Some users of this system prefer to add another rating of "very important" between "mandatory" and "important." In that case "very important" gets the 3 rating, and "mandatory" is rated 4.)

The importance of the relationship between each two spaces is decided and recorded, in number rating, on the spatial allocation diagram just shown. The diagram provides a synopsis of all spatial relationships—the essence of the entire program—on a single sheet. Clusters of highly related spaces become obvious.

We'll see how you objectively decide the importance of the spatial relationships a little further on. Right now, we'll consider how to apply the data you gain from a spatial allocation diagram to the bubble diagram system described at the beginning of the chapter.

The steps are essentially the same as described in the previous section on how to find plan conflicts. In the first example, we didn't consider differences in importance of room relationships. This time the importance will be shown by labeling line connections in the bubble diagram with the appropriate number from the spatial allocation diagram. The lines labeled "3" and "2" are given first priority in length reduction as the bubble diagram is untangled and redrawn. Undesirable relationships should be drawn in red line dashes. Where conflicts arise in later plan development, the chart provides clear standards for deciding which aspects of the plan are most important and which compromises are most acceptable.

Site relationships aren't shown in these examples, but site features of view, access, utility service, etc., should all be listed on the original spatial allocation diagram.

Some further points of advice are:

- The final bubble diagram is often very revealing and may be taken as a literal final plan. This may be an error. The diagram based on the spatial allocation diagram shows correct relationships between rooms, but the same relationships may be possible in varying ways. The diagram provides the best possible basis for a successful plan, but it isn't necessarily the plan in itself.

- It simplifies matters if you group obviously closely related spaces as single units. And you can ignore the smallest minor spaces. That way you will reduce the total number of bubbles to be manipulated. When you have over 20 spaces in 1 diagram with a multitude of relationships, the untangling process gets unnecessarily tedious.

Here's a way to augment the usefulness and accuracy of the spatial allocation diagram:

- You can divide chart grids in half and insert a code letter along with numerical rankings, to identify *why* an evaluation was made. Write down reasons for relationships as they are stated during planning meetings and number them. This becomes a legend of reasons with explanatory notes, and the numbers become reference keys to add to the spatial allocation diagram relationship ratings. A partial example follows:

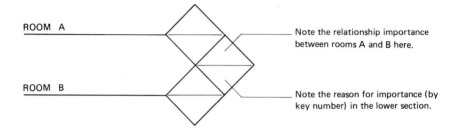

ROOM A — Note the relationship importance between rooms A and B here.

ROOM B — Note the reason for importance (by key number) in the lower section.

The identification guards against memory lapses, assists double-checking for errors, and allows quick reevaluation when the planning process bogs down or when conflicts are discovered later.

HOW TO COMPUTE PLAN QUALITY MATHEMATICALLY

The spatial allocation diagram provides a quick and effective method for mathematically comparing and judging different floor plans. The method has been incorporated in some computer-aided design programs, but can be applied accurately with a calculator or paper and pencil. The system incorporates a standard of judgment based on the premise that, all other things being equal, the best plan is one that minimizes the most distances between related spaces. This is easy to measure and score. Only two measurements are combined: the importance rankings on the spatial allocation diagram and the distances between spaces.

The distances between spaces may be measured in feet or module units, whichever is most convenient. And measurement may be taken from room-to-room centers of gravity, from circulation paths to room centers, or just between points of access. These decisions may depend upon the building functions and ease of computation; the only absolute requirement is that you remain consistent in whatever measurement system you decide upon.

With that decided, the rest is easy.

Multiply each measurement of distance between related rooms by the numerical ranking of the importance of that relationship.

Place the resulting figure in a slot in a chart like the spatial diagram illustrated earlier. Instead of making a mark to show that there is some relationship, you provide a number to show the importance or ranking of that relationship. Where a relationship is inconsequential, you make no calculation and place a zero in the chart.

You can usually ignore negative relationships; it's generally faster to keep them out of the calculation, but just be sure spaces that must be kept away from each other are adequately separated in all the plan options under consideration.

When you've multiplied relationship rankings by distances for all related rooms, add up all the products for a total overall score of the plan. The plan with the lowest total score—the lowest sum of products of distance times value rankings—is the one that provides the best total spatial and functional efficiency.

The final evaluation is only as good as the criteria and the accuracy of previous evaluations of room relationships. If you don't like the plan that comes out best numerically, you may have to take another look at the evaluation system.

Some designers wonder why a simple measurement and total of distances, alone, won't show the most economical spatial groupings. The reason is that it's less important that rooms with lower ranking relationships be close. For example, a 20-foot distance between rooms with a "very important" relationship ranking would be multiplied by 3 for a product of 60; the same distance for two rooms with an "important" ranking would be multiplied by 2 for a product of 40. The difference between 60 and 40 represents the fact that it's more important that the rooms with a 3 relationship be close together; any distance between these rooms should be penalized more than the same distance between rooms with lower importance rankings.

Users of this scoring system consider it indispensable for showing themselves and their clients the specific merits of one scheme over another. But it has a few dangers.

When a designer simply "likes" one plan more than another, she or he may consciously or unconsciously fudge the numbers to corroborate personal judgment. Having the scoring done by someone other than the designer may improve accuracy. If considerations exist that should override spatial efficiency, they should be examined, evaluated, given numerical weights and included as part of the criteria for comparing plan options.

The diagrams and scoring system have been described for two-dimensional plans. How do you handle three-dimensional (3-D), multistory construction? Usually, you can work with single clusters of rooms on a floor-by-floor basis without worrying about their relationships to the floor above or below. Where there are 3-D relationships to contend with, some designers resort to three-dimensional-model versions of the link and node diagram and the bubble diagram. And computer software that can be run on microcomputers is coming on the market shortly that will expedite such work.

IMPROVING THE ACCURACY OF PLAN QUALITY COMPUTATIONS

You can rapidly calculate plan efficiency with the spatial allocation diagram as just described. But the accuracy of calculation depends on sound initial judgment of room-to-room proximity ratings.

Often there's no problem at all in rating a relationship. Most, if not all, "mandatory" room connections are self-evident. In a school, gymnasium storage goes with the gym; there will be a service driveway and trash pickup by the cafeteria; and so forth. Rooms that have no relationship to one another are also usually self-evident.

The fastest way to evaluate all room relationships is to let the client go through the allocation diagram and mark down judgments, along with notes of reasons for the judgments. If the client can't decide on something, ask him or her to skip over it. After discussing the pros and cons of some of the decisions, repeat the run-through. By this time the project as a whole will be far better understood than before, and the client can decide some previously undecided points and change some of the preliminary evaluations. A lot of "very important" relationships will turn out to be "unimportant," and so on.

If the importance rating of some spatial relationship is still undecided after the second-stage evaluation process, you can apply formulas to help nail down a decision.

The following provides a calculation you can use in relationship evaluation. It may appear complex at first reading, but it is fast, easy to use, and very rewarding in terms of expediting planning decisions.

1. Estimate the volume of traffic or communication between two spaces as "high," "medium," or "low."

2. Estimate the frequency of interaction as "high," "medium," or "low."

3. Estimate the relative cost or value of the personnel involved, or of the interaction, as "high," "medium," or "low."

4. Give numerical values of 3, 2, and 1 to the respective high, medium, and low evaluations. Multiply the values for volume, frequency, and cost to get a ranking of the importance of the relationship. For example, if the volume, frequency, and cost of interaction between the spaces are all "high," the values are 3 × 3 × 3, for a product of 27. If two are "high," but one is "medium," the values are 3 × 3 × 2, which equals 18.

The possible total values are 27, 18, 12, 8, 4, 2, or 1. A total of 27 indicates a "very important" relationship. This would be translated as 3 on the weighted spatial allocation diagram. Values of 18 and 12 indicate an "important" relationship, whereas 8 and 4 suggest a "desirable" relationship, and 2 and 1 are "unimportant."

There are more elaborate and precise evaluative formulas, but this one has the advantages of speed and simplicity. Its results usually coincide with more sophisticated techniques.

If, after using the breakdown shown here, there is still doubt— for whatever reason—you can make a compromise relationship evaluation. You can rank a relationship on the weighted spatial allocation diagram as an in-between number. The value that is in between "desirable" and "important" would be between 1 and 2, or 1.5. This kind of compromise helps resolve time-consuming vacillations and keeps the process moving along.

THE "PROTO-PLAN" SYSTEM

"Proto-planning" (a plan for planning) is a successful timesaving refinement upon some of the systems described earlier in this chapter. It's the invention of your author. When I first proposed it for a programming course at the College of Environmental Design at the University of California, Berkeley, I wrote:

I wanted a means of relating a lot of different considerations in one operation. Besides relating the rooms properly, I wanted to tie in all important site relationships along with them. Also, I felt that each interior and exterior element should be worked in with one another and with all the other elements as a group. In other words each room has some relationship with the exterior, a relationship with specific rooms, and a relationship to the building as a whole. I needed a system for dealing with all three types of relationships simultaneously.

The system starts with a "plan control chart." When the chart is filled in, the user counts the total number or the total importance rankings of relationships for each building space. This tells the "planning importance" of each space.

This is different from the types of evaluation previously described. For example, a kitchen in a residence often has the greatest total number of relationships with other spaces, and their importance ranking usually totals to the highest number. This gives the kitchen the highest planning importance, although it wouldn't necessarily be considered the most important room of the building.

Rooms with the highest planning importance will have a central position relative to other spaces. Rooms with the lowest planning importance will be peripheral spaces. This evaluation provides the first clue for the best final general disposition of all spaces.

Planning importance rankings are written beside the name of each space on the plan control chart. The space (or spaces) with the highest planning importance is noted as "1." The next highest ranking space (or spaces) is noted as "2," and so on. (The plan control chart includes all appropriate site spaces: yards, street, drives, view area, etc., and these receive their planning importance ratings along with the interior spaces.)

An abstract site plan is prepared on grid paper. Actual site boundaries are not scaled and drawn, but compass directions, view, access directions, etc., are noted.

Cardboard squares or rectangles representing building spaces are drawn to small scale and cut out. These are placed on the grid in sequence of importance. The space with the highest planning importance rating (a ranking of 1) is set dead center on the grid. If there are two or more spaces with the number 1 rank, they are set adjacent to each other in the center.

The second-highest planning importance space or spaces (a ranking of 2) is set adjacent to the number 1 space. It may go above or below, left or right, depending on any relationship to site factors. If no site relationship exists for the number 2 space, it may be set tentatively directly above or below the number 1 space.

The number 2 space now has a square "orbit," a band equal to its width, extending around the central space. It can be moved within this band when later adjustments are made.

The number 3 space is placed just outside the orbit of the number 2 space, and to the right or left, up or down, as required by site relationships. If no site relationships exist, it, too, can be placed directly upward or downward from the center.

All other cardboard "rooms" are located through this sequence. When two or more have the same planning importance, they will share the same orbit. Otherwise each space has its own band which represents its planning importance relationship with all other spaces. The diagram below illustrates the abstract site plan.

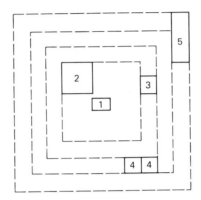

When completed, the abstract site plan shows a floor plan that is literally exploded. Rooms are scattered in all directions in accordance with their relationship to *exterior* factors. The next step is to pull the rooms together in accordance with *interior* relationships. This task has been simplified by the foregoing steps.

A bubble sketch is made of the cardboard layout. Relationship lines and numerical rankings, as described on page 23, are drawn to connect the bubbles. (The "bubbles" may be drawn as scaled rooms; this sometimes aids visualization.) Many overly long or crossed lines which normally appear in the first bubble diagram of a plan will not occur in this sketch. The layout process can usually be eliminated by moving the rooms around within their orbits.

Once rooms are adjusted diagrammatically to eliminate interior plan conflicts, all that is left is to shorten connective lines by pulling the rooms inward from their orbits toward the central rooms to which they relate the most. The distance between rooms with the strongest relationships is reduced first; the rest follow in order. What remains is a diagrammatic outline which will suggest the most workable options for the final plan. The most promising of these options can then be sketched to scale and compared for efficiency according to plan evaluation methods described on pages 26 through 27.

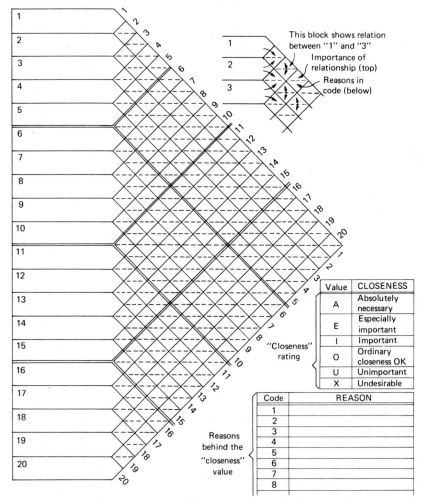

Figure 2.1 Another version of a *relationship matrix* or *spatial interaction diagram*. (Courtesy of CalComp.)

Figure 2.2 An electronic version of a *spatial relationship matrix* as shown on the computer screen. A color code is provided along with numbers to indicate the degree and/or importance of the interaction between the listed building areas. (Courtesy of CalComp.)

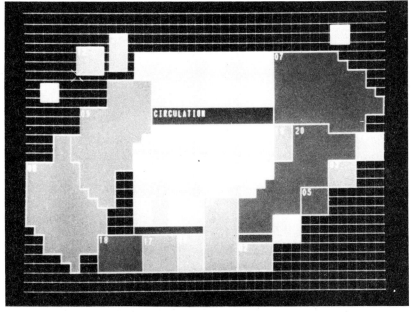

Figure 2.3 The computer ranks the relative success of optional schemes by combining factors such as the number of interactions and their importance, just as in the simple example explained in this chapter. Spaces are moved about and tested in different combinations and relationships until you get the best"score." Different space types are color-coded on the screen and will be plotted out in color for study and presentation. (Courtesy of CalComp.)

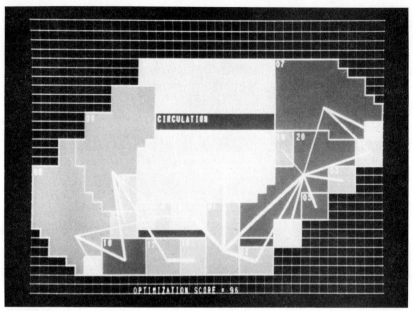

Figure 2.4 The computer image *blocking diagram* shows the functions and spaces of one floor of a building according to the relationships established in the spatial relationship matrix. The amount of interaction between spaces is indicated by the thickness of lines that connect the centers of related spaces. (Courtesy of CalComp.)

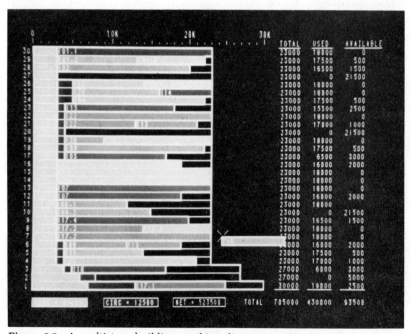

Figure 2.5 A multistory building *stacking diagram* on the computer screen. It shows what space is being used on each level, what types of spaces they are, and how much leftover space, if any, is available on each floor. (Courtesy of CalComp.)

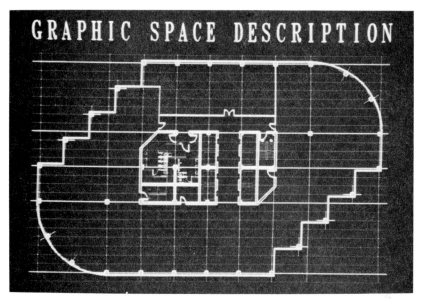

Figure 2.6 Here the abstract spatial relationship matrix and blocking diagram become expressed as the beginnings of a tangible floor plan. (Courtesy of CalComp.)

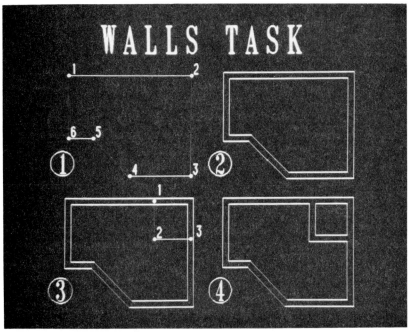

Figure 2.7 As the plan is firmed up, operators start inserting real building fixtures from the CADD menu, such as these walls. (Courtesy of CalComp.)

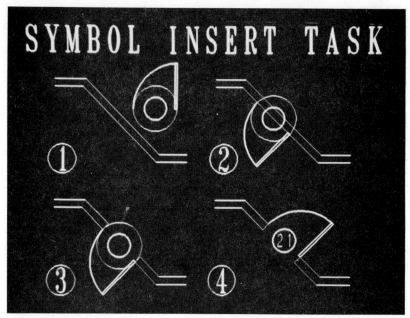

Figure 2.8 After walls are in, openings and inserted fixtures such as doors and door symbols are inputted by the CADD operator. (Courtesy of CalComp.)

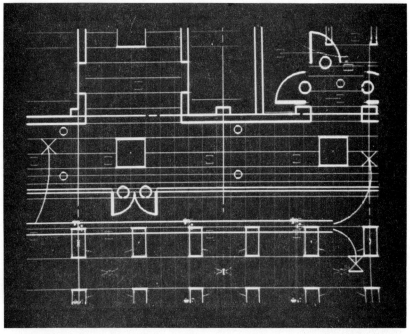

Figure 2.9 The formerly abstract and schematic floor plan now takes on the characteristics of a preliminary working drawing. Each category of information is created on a separate electronic "overlay." The exterior walls are one layer, interior partitions are another, ceiling fixtures are another, and so on. (Courtesy of CalComp.)

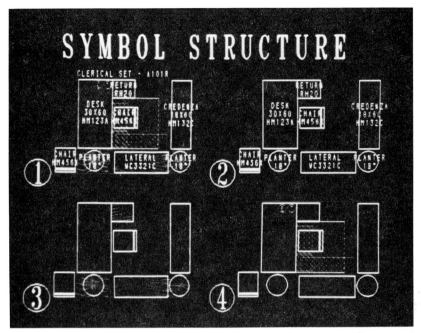

Figure 2.10 Interior design components such as low-height partitions, planters, and furnishings are stored and categorized in the CADD system's electronic file. (Courtesy of CalComp.)

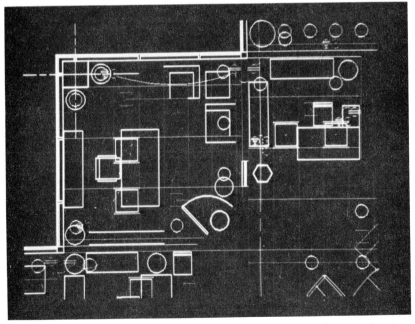

Figure 2.11 Furnishings are moved into position and electronically "pasted up" on their own CADD overlay sheet. (Courtesy of CalComp.)

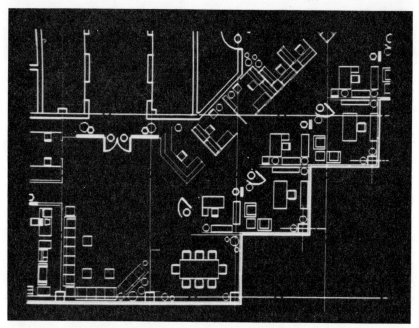

Figure 2.12 This zoom-away view shows several layers of floor plan information including one optional furniture arrangement. (Courtesy of CalComp.)

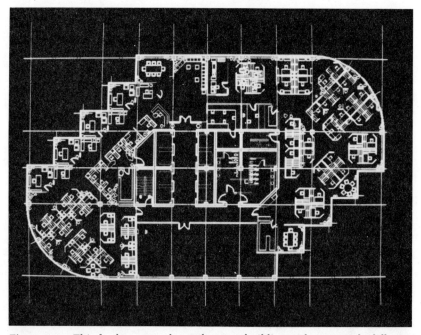

Figure 2.13 This further zoom shows the same building with an entirely different furniture arrangement. Any number of alternative interior plans can be tested with the overall building plan without having to redraw the overall plan each time. (Courtesy of CalComp.)

Speaking of Planning, What Is a "Plan"?

"A plan is when you get tired of planning."
—Murphy's Mimic

Historically, the word "plan" shares origins with the word "plain"—from the Latin *planus,* for flat or level. From historical reference it implies a two-dimensional existence. The word "map" has similar experiential origins, being from the Latin *mappa,* a cloth upon which maps were drawn.

Mapping, charting, or diagramming is the evident origin of the process we now call "planning." That is, after people had the experience of creating an abstract, small-scale visual representation of some part of the world—a map—someone realized they could reverse the process. Besides mapping what is, they could map what isn't. They could invent a map of what might be. And if they could do that, they could invent events that might be. They could draw speculative movements of people and goods on the map. That was the first version of what we now call playing "what if."

Similarly, along came "modeling." The concept "model" is from the Latin *modus,* which means a "measure." Early models were of real things—the Egyptians made miniatures of all aspects of human work and play. And there were models of imagined things, such as the icons, statuettes, and enshrined images that guided the lives of ancient Mediterraneans. (A characteristic of ancient Egyptian culture was the belief that a word or hieroglyph was not just symbolic but actually equal to the thing it represented, at least in the realm of the spirit.)

Once people were used to making representational and symbolic models, the next step was to use models to represent that which did not yet exist but which could be made to exist for some desired purpose. Then, by modeling with parts

37

and pieces, they could move things around and get a small-scale representation of what would happen if they took this or that course of action in the real world without actually taking that action. "What if," again.

Historically, the first maps and plans were mainly military—for exploration, conquest, and defense. Generals created models or maps of battle situations and moved things around that model as an imitation of reality. By imitating reality in miniature, they perceived that they could simulate real events and their consequences. They could compare the likely consequences of one set of actions as opposed to another. This was planning in the modern sense: goal-directed, conscious, comparative in terms of options, and "modeled."

Modeling is one of those great breakthroughs, a classic conceptual leap that moves a whole culture forward. It started with the equally hot idea of "mapping." When human beings discovered the concept of linear measurement, they simultaneously discovered that they could measure land and recreate the measurements in miniature, as drawings, where a small unit such as an inch could represent a larger unit such as a mile. That way they could make vastly huge and almost incomprehensible things small and manageable. In fact, they could take things that were so large they were beyond immediate human perception—continents and oceans—and make them small enough to be immediately graspable by the human mind.

That's "scaling," the proportional measurement that is essential to all graphic plans and 3-D models. The idea is so ingrained now that when people use the word "model," they usually precede the term with the word "scale."

The great first conceptual leap in planning was to make huge complex things small and abstract so that the mind could take them in. The next great step was a reversal—to make small-scale models of nonexistent things in order to figure out how to make them real, and of real-life size.

Modeling comes in several versions. There's literal 3-D physical modeling, such as used by many designers. There's sketch and drawing modeling. There's verbal modeling. And mathematical modeling. They all deal with recreating reality in a miniature of abstract form. They're all means of identifying and comparing various options for action. What's also intriguing and of ultimate value to us is that these are all methods for solving problems.[1]

To solve a problem means to do two things:

1. Reduce the problem situation to an abstract form—a model.

2. Modify the model's parts, attributes, and related circumstances until you simulate—in abstraction or in miniature—something that will fulfill the need, identify the unknown, resolve the conflict, etc., as required to respond to whatever prompted the problem-solving process.

---

[1]Historically, one of the primary uses of tools is to make more tools. Hence, abstract modeling is now used not just to solve problems, plan buildings, and the like, but to establish plans and methods for improving the planning process. One of the fascinating uses of contemporary problem-solving methods is their application to the problem of how best to solve problems.

Now a key point emerges.

If planning and modeling require tools of abstraction and miniaturization, then the abstracts and miniatures have to be accurate—faithful to what they represent. If the model of the existing situation is accurate, then it can be manipulated successfully to achieve whatever you desire in terms of solution. If it is not accurate, all the manipulation in the world will not achieve a realistic situation. Often models are not accurate. Often they are incomplete, or falsified.

This is the area where many, possibly most, architectural designers and planners falter. It is the reason so many buildings and designs fail to do their specified job. It's the reason so many buildings stand as random objects, not functional, not stimulating, not beautiful.

chapter 3

Space Planning Rules of Thumb

"Rules of thumb may lead to the same mistakes as long tedious calculations, but you get to quit work sooner."

—Murphy

RULES OF THUMB FOR ESTIMATING ROOM AND SPACE SIZES

When you have estimates of how many people will be using a facility, you can size site and building spaces during the preliminary design according to the following rules of thumb.

Parking Areas, Driveways, and Walks

Preliminary Parking Layouts

- Total parking areas, including walks and driveways: estimate at about 400 square feet per car. (Tight planning can reduce this to 300 square feet.)
- Typical parking stall: 9 × 16 feet = 144 square feet total

Driveways

- Minimum clear width of drive at parallel parking: 20 feet, 18-foot minimum for two-way traffic if there's no parking along the sides.

- Two-way drive between 45 or 60° parking stalls: should be at least 22 feet wide.

- One-way or two-way drive between 90° parking stalls: should be at least 28 feet wide.

- One-way drives, including those with angled parking on one side: may be 12 feet clear in width.

- Maximum recommended grade for driveways: 5 percent or ⅝ inch per foot.

- Minimum drainage slope for parking areas: 1 percent, or ⅛ inch per foot.

Walkways

- Main walkways for large buildings require minimum clear widths of from 6 to 8 feet. Main walkways for small buildings and subsidiary walks for larger buildings are typically 3 to 5 feet in width. Walks adjacent to parking areas where bumpers overhang the walk should be at least 6 feet wide.

- Maximum walkway slope: 1 in 8. Handrails are required for greater slope. Maximum slope with handrails: 1 in 10. If steps occur along walkways, at least three risers are required. Handrails are provided for steps over three risers.

Occupancies

Occupant Loads According to Room or Building Type

These estimates of occupancies are in agreement with most building codes. The figures are used to estimate room sizes, elevator loads, mechanical and plumbing requirements, and design of corridors, stairs, and exits. Remember, these are minimal requirements, not optimal:

- Auditoriums and assembly rooms: 7 square feet per person with fixed seating; 15 square feet per person with movable seating.

- Classrooms: 20 square feet per person. (Some codes require 40 square feet.)

- Commercial buildings, stores: 30 square feet per person for basement and ground floor; 60 square feet per person for upper floors.
- Conference and dining rooms: 15 square feet per person.
- Clinics, wards: three visitors per bed space.
- Private hospitals: 1.5 visitors per bed space.
- Hotels: 1.5 persons per bedroom.
- Housing, multiunit: two to three persons per unit.
- Housing, low-rent: three to four persons per unit.
- Housing, single-family: minimum 150 square feet per habitable room per person.
- Libraries: 50 square feet per person.
- Lounges, lobbies: 15 square feet per person.
- Offices: 100 square feet of office space per person; clerical pools: 50 to 75 square feet per person.
- Theater foyers: 3 square feet per person.

Corridors, Exits, and Stairs

Corridor Widths

Usual range of corridor widths:

- Commercial, office, dormitories: 5 to 7 feet.
- Medical buildings, laboratories: 8 to 10 feet.
- Schools: 8 to 12 feet.
- Apartments, hotels: 3 feet, 6 inches minimum for service corridors and bedroom hallways; 5 to 7 feet for public corridors—12 percent wider at elevators.

Exit Corridors—Minimum Widths

Required widths vary according to local ordinances, but the following rules are based on common practice and will serve for preliminary planning:

- Minimum width of any corridor serving as required exit for occupant load over 10: at least 44 inches wide.
- Total width (in feet) of exits equals the maximum total occupant load divided by 50. Any single exit door has clear opening of at least 34 inches.

Dead-End Corridor Length

- Maximum allowable length of dead-end corridors or exterior exit balconies: 20 feet.

Maximum Distance to Exits

- Distance to outside or to exit corridor or stair in unsprinklered buildings: 150 feet maximum.
- Distance in sprinklered buildings: 200 feet, maximum.
- Distance from living unit entries to elevators: 180 feet, maximum.

Auditorium Exits

See AUDITORIUMS, page 45.

Minimum Number of Exits

- Where supervision is required in exiting, such as in hospitals and day care centers: provide two exits for any room with occupant load of five or more.
- For residential occupancies, such as hotels, dormitories, dwellings: provide two exits for any space with occupancy of 10 or more.
- Stores, auditoriums, and miscellaneous assembly areas: provide two exits for every 50 occupants.
- As with exit corridors, the usual minimum total width (in feet) of exits equals the maximum total occupancy divided by 50.

Exit Stair Widths

- Stair widths follow according to corridor and exit width requirements as previously described.
- Otherwise, commonly used minimum widths are:
  - Private stair, occupant load under 10: 30 inches.
  - Public stair, occupant load of 50 or fewer: 36 inches.
  - Public stair, occupant load over 50: 44 inches.
- Handrails: provided on both sides of public stairs.
- Maximum distance between handrails on wide stairways: 4 feet, 4 inches.

Auditoriums

Auditorium Sizing

- In planning audience seating area according to anticipated occupancy, assume 7 square feet of floor space per person for fixed seating, 15 square feet per person for movable seats.
- Stage and backstage areas are often equal to the ground floor auditorium seating area. Lobbies often equal about 30 percent of auditorium seating area. These proportions vary enormously according to auditorium use, but can serve as preliminary assumptions.

Seating

- Seating rows: spaced back-to-back at minimum of 33 inches. For continental seating, the clear width between seats in up position and backs of forward row should be at least 22 inches.
- Minimum seat width: 18 inches; 20 to 22 inches is recommended.

Aisles

- Narrowest width of aisle furthest from exit serving one side of seating: 3 feet; serving two sides, minimum width: 3 feet, 6 inches.
- Aisle widths: Increase by 1½ inches for each 5 feet of distance from narrowest point toward exit or cross aisle.
- Continental seating aisles: minimum 44 inches wide.

Aisle Spacing

- Standard seating limitation of building codes specifies a maximum of six seats between any seat and the closest aisle. Inside rows this permits a maximum of seven seats to aisle; middle seating sections have a maximum of 13 seats between aisles.
- Continental seating row lengths: limited to 29 intervening seats from any one seat.

Auditorium Exits

- Main exits should be equal in width to total width of aisles, passages, and stairs. In addition, main exit total width should have capacity equal to half the total maximum auditorium occupancy load.

- Side exits to be reached by side aisles or cross aisles should provide a total width adequate to carry one-third of the total maximum occupancy.

- Continental seating requires one pair of side doors for each five rows of seats. Minimum exit clear widths are 66 inches per exit.

Elevators

Elevator Car Capacities

- Assume a normal passenger load of 10 persons for a 2000-pound-capacity elevator car. Add three passengers for each additional 500 pounds of elevator car capacity.

Elevator Hoistway Sizes

- For preliminary planning, assume 6-foot, 6-inch front-to-back clear hoistway for a 2500-pound-capacity car.

- Add 6 inches to the front-to-back dimension for each additional 500 pounds of car capacity.

- Assume 17 feet total width for each pair of elevator hoistways for cars up to 3500-pound capacity. At 4000 pounds, assume a 19-foot-wide hoistway for each pair of cars.

Preliminary Estimate of Elevator Requirements

For quick estimating, assume the following:

- Waiting time interval: 30 seconds.
- Car capacity: 3000 pounds (normal load, 16 passengers).
- Car speed: 700 feet per minute for office building; minimum of 300 feet per minute for other buildings.
- Service capacity: adequate to carry 13 percent of building occupancy in 5 minutes.

If building size, number of stories, and occupancy are known, rough estimates of elevator requirements can be computed according to the foregoing standards.

Elevator Lobby Size

- Allow 4 square feet per person for occupancy spread out over 20 minutes each of peak morning and afternoon load times.
- Another rule: Assume 6- to 9-foot-wide lobby for elevators at one side; 10 to 12 feet for elevators, both sides.

Mechanical

Mechanical Space

- Using a commercial office building as a median example, total mechanical space will usually be around 5 to 10 percent of the total gross building area.
- Total mechanical space for laboratories and hospitals will be from 25 to 50 percent higher than for office buildings. Total mechanical space for simpler, low-occupancy, open-plan buildings may be around 30 percent lower than for office buildings.

(Rules of thumb in use for estimating mechanical needs vary considerably among specialists in the field. Rules presented here are generalized and intended only as sketch aids during schematic and early preliminary phases of planning and design.)

Shafts—Heating and Air-Conditioning

- For a preliminary estimate, take estimated air quantity in cubic feet per minute (cfm), divide by 1000, and multiply the result by 1.3. The final figure gives the approximate square footage of vertical air duct shaft space required.
- Another rule for estimating square footage of shaft space required: allow 35 to 60 square feet for each 1000 cfm of supply air furnished. Use lower or higher square feet figures according to the simplicity or complexity of the system.
- Overall, expect from 2 to 5 percent of the total floor area (or up to 50 percent of the total mechanical space) to be taken by heating and air-conditioning shafts.
- Air supply shafts are usually centralized, serving floor space within from 50 to 100 feet from the shaft.

Shafts—Proportioning

- Rectangular duct shafts prove most practical when proportioned within the range of from 2 to 1 through 4 to 1.

Shafts—Electrical and Plumbing

- Nontechnical buildings: expect up to 1 to 1.5 percent of floor space to be taken up with electrical and plumbing chases or shafts. Space for each is about equal. Electrical shafts near elevator shafts or stairwells often cause congestion in floor and ceiling wiring, so other locations should be considered.

Air-Conditioning Plant Size

- Needs about 0.3 cubic feet of space per each cfm of air exchanged. This works out to about 100 cubic feet of space required per ton of refrigeration, assuming approximately 350 cfm per ton.
- Secondary fan rooms take about 0.25 cubic feet of space per cfm of air handled.
- One mechanical room usually serves about twelve stories, but sometimes serves up to twenty stories.

Air-Conditioning—Outside Air Duct

- Assume 8 square feet of air duct for the first 5000 square feet of building floor area, and double that for each doubling in size of floor space.

Fan Room Space and Ceiling Height

- Fan rooms take a large portion of total mechanical space—3 to 7 percent of gross building area. Allow from 16 to 18 feet of ceiling height.

Cooling Tower Space

- General rule: Allow 1 square foot of roof area per each 400 square feet of total building area. Towers range from 13 to 40 feet in height.

- Another useful rule: Allow 1 square foot of tower space per ton of refrigeration. In finding ton capacity, assume 320 cfm per ton for electric drive refrigeration or 540 cfm per ton of steam drive refrigeration.

Heating Plant

- Two boilers are usually provided; sizes range from 4 to 1C feet wide, 10 to 30 feet long, with ample walkaround space and tube pulling space equal to boiler length in front of fire tube boilers.
- Boiler room ceilings range from 12 to 22 feet high.
- Chimney sizes range from 3 to about 8 feet in diameter.
- Assume smaller or larger plants depending on the size and complexity of the project.

Plumbing

Toilet Rooms

- Assume approximately 50 square feet of total toilet room space per water closet.

Water Closets—Minimum Allocation of Fixtures

- Auditoriums: 1 per 100 persons. If occupant load is over 400, add 1 for each additional 500 males, 1 for each additional 100 females.
- Dormitories: 1 per 8 males, 1 for each 4 females.
- Office and institutional buildings: 1 for each 15 persons up to 50 occupants; 1 per 20 persons up to 100 occupants; 1 for each 40 additional persons. Multiply these estimates by 1.5 for female occupancy.
- Industrial plants, laboratories, shops: 1 per 10 persons up to 50 occupants; 1 per 20 persons up to 100 occupants; 1 for each additional 30 occupants. Multiply these estimates by 1.5 for female occupancy.
- Schools: 1 per 100 males; 1 per 20 females.

Lavatories—Minimum Allocation of Fixtures

- Auditoriums: 1 per 100 persons. If occupancy is over 750, add 1 per each 500 persons.
- Dormitories: 1 per 15 persons.
- Office and institutional buildings: 1 per 15 persons for occupant load up to 60; 1 per 25 persons for occupant load up to 125; 1 for each additional 45 persons.
- Industrial plants, laboratories, shops: 1 per 10 persons.
- Schools: 1 per 60 to 100 persons.

Urinals—Minimum Allocation of Fixtures

- Auditoriums: 1 per each 100 males; if male occupancy is over 500, add 1 for each additional 300 males.
- Other buildings: 1 per 25 males.

Showers

- Dormitories, shops, industrial plants: 1 per 10 persons.
- Coed or women's dormitories: 1 per 8 persons.
- Occupant loads over 150: add 1 for each additional 20 persons.

Toilet Room Plumbing Chase Sizes

These are minimums; main risers are not provided for:

- Lavatory, single, one side: 3-inch clear space.
- Lav gang, one side: 8 inches.
- Lav gang, two sides: 10 to 12 inches.
- Urinal, single, one side: 6 inches.
- Urinals, gang, one side: 8 inches.
- Urinals, gang, two sides: 12 inches.
- Water closet, single, one side: 8 inches.
- Water closets, gang, one side: 12 inches.
- Water closets, gang, two sides: 18 to 24 inches.
- Combination wall, lavs, or urinals on one side and water closets on other side: allow 14 to 18 inches.

- Combination wall, lavs on one side and urinals on other side: allow 12-inch chase clear space.

RULES OF THUMB FOR PRELIMINARY STRUCTURAL DESIGN

Most designers rely on common rules of thumb when they make preliminary tentative decisions on construction, framing, and structural systems. The rules are especially useful in making rough estimates of what framing can be used for certain required spans. And as an aid to estimating building heights, the rules are helpful in gauging the depths of various kinds of framing.

Most structural rules of thumb are expressed as ratios. For example, a truss may be estimated as having a span-to-depth ratio of 8. As long as depths and spans are expressed in terms of feet, that relationship is easy to perceive. In the truss example, the truss will be about 1 foot deep for every 8 feet of span.

Many ratios are expressed in terms of spans in feet, but with the framing member thicknesses or depths in inches. Those require a little extra calculation. For example, if a beam has a span-to-depth ratio of 20 and you want to know the likely depth in inches for a 25-foot span, take the following steps:

1. Translate the span footage into inches: 25 feet $\times$ 12 = 300 inches
2. Divide the span in inches by the ratio 20: 300 inches $\div$ 20 = 15 inches

The estimated depth of the beam for that span using the given ratio is 15 inches.

Alternatively, you can work with decimals and divide the span in feet by the ratio:

25-foot span $\div$ span-to-depth ratio of 20 = 1.25 feet

This, of course, is the same result as given by the previous calculation, a beam depth of 1 foot, 3 inches, or 15 inches.

Rules of thumb can't be taken seriously beyond the first preliminary estimating stages of design. They're fine for establishing general limits, but staff must be discouraged from using them as substitutes for actual structural engineering.

RULES OF THUMB FOR TYPICAL SPANS AND SIZES

Concrete

Precast Concrete Plank Floor System: 8- to 36-Foot Spans (up to 60 Feet for Long Span)

- Typical thicknesses: 4 to 20 inches in 2-inch increments, plus 1½-inch concrete topping
- Typical span-to-depth ratio: 35

Reinforced Concrete Beams: 10- to 40-Foot Spans

- Typical thicknesses: 8 to 12 inches
- Typical span-to-depth ratios: 12 to 16
- For average beam, span in feet equals depth in inches

Prestressed Concrete I Beams: 20- to 100-Foot Spans

- Typical thicknesses: 12 to 16 inches
- Typical span-to-depth ratios: 20 to 25

Prestressed Concrete T Beams: 20- to 120-Foot Spans

- Typical thicknesses: 8- to 10-inch flange widths, web thickness of 8 inches
- Typical span-to-depth ratio: 30

Precast Reinforced Concrete Joists: 20- to 45-Foot Spans

- Typical span-to-depth ratios: 20 to 24

Prestressed Concrete Joists: 40- to 60-Foot Spans

- Typical span-to-depth ratio: 32

Reinforced Concrete Slab on Steel Beams: 20-Foot Span

- Typical maximum beam spacing: 8 feet
- Typical slab thickness: 4 inches

Reinforced Concrete Waffle Slab: 25- to 40-Foot Spans

- Standard pan sizes: 20 and 30 inches square with other sizes available
- Standard pan depths: 8 to 14 inches in 2-inch increments
- Typical span-to-depth ratio: 25

Reinforced Concrete Flat Slab with Drop Panels: 16- to 36-Foot Spans

- Typical thicknesses: 6 to 12 inches
- Typical maximum ratio of long to short side of bay: 1.33
- Side dimension of drop panel: one-third of span
- Typical span-to-depth ratio: 36

Reinforced Concrete Flat Plate Slab: 10- to 30-Foot Spans

- Typical thicknesses: 6 to 10 inches
- Typical maximum ratio of long to short side of bay: 1.33
- Typical span-to-depth ratio: 30

A common rule is to allow 1 inch of thickness for each 3 feet of span.

Steel

Cellular Steel Floor: 8 to 16 Feet (up to 32 Feet for Long Span)

- Typical thicknesses: 1½ to 6 inches, plus 2½-inch concrete topping
- Typical span-to-depth ratio: 50

Steel Beams: 10- to 60-Foot Spans

- Typical steel frame bay sizes: 20 to 24 feet
- Typical span-to-depth ratio: 20

(Roof beams, depth of beam in inches = 0.4 $\times$ span in feet; floor beams, depth of beam in inches = 0.6 $\times$ span in feet.)

Steel Plate Girders: 20- to 80-Foot Spans

- Typical span-to-depth ratio: 14

Steel Joists: 8- to 48-Foot Spans (up to 96 Feet for Long Span Joists)

- Typical spacings: 24 inches at floors, 30 inches at roofs
- Typical span-to-depth ratios: 20 to 24

The maximum for estimating floor joist depths is 20; the maximum for estimating depths of roof joists is 24. Joists are in 2-inch increments from 8 to 24 inches deep and 18 to 48 inches for long span types.

Flat or Arched Steel Trusses: 30- to 220-Foot Spans

- Typical spacings: 12 to 20 feet
- Typical span-to-depth ratio: 12

Triangular Steel Trusses: 30- to 150-Foot Spans

- Typical spacings: 12 to 20 feet
- Typical span-to-depth ratios: 7 to 8

Wood

Wood Plank Floor System: 4- to 22-Foot Spans

- Typical thicknesses: 2 to 4 inches
- Typical span-to-depth ratio: 48

Solid Wood Beams: 8- to 32-Foot Spans

- Typical spacings: 4 to 20 feet
- Typical thicknesses: 2 to 14 inches
- Typical span-to-depth ratios: 16 to 20

Solid Wood Girders
Glu-Lam Beams: 16- to 50-Foot Spans

- Typical spacings: 4 to 20 feet
- Typical thicknesses: 3¼ to 9 inches
- Typical span-to-depth ratio: 24
- Typical ratio of beam depth to width: 2 to 1 for light beams, 3 to 1 for large members

Wood Floor Joists: 8- to 25-Foot Spans

- Typical spacing: 16 inches
- Typical span-to-depth ratio: 20

Wood Roof Joists, Ceiling Joists, Rafters: 8- to 25-Foot Spans

- Typical spacings: 16 to 24 inches

(Multiply span in feet by 0.5 for estimate of joist depth in inches, then round upwards to nearest 2-inch increment.)

Flat Wood Trusses: 40- to 160-Foot Spans

- Typical spacings: 12 to 20 feet
- Typical depth-to-span ratio: 1 to 10

Triangular Wood Trusses: 40- to 100-Foot Spans

- Typical spacings: 12 to 20 feet
- Typical depth-to-span ratio: 1 to 6

Bowstring Trusses: 40- to 200-Foot Spans

- Typical spacings: 12 to 20 feet
- Typical depth-to-span ratios: 1 to 6 and 1 to 8

Two- and Three-Hinge Wood Arches: 20- to 150-Foot Spans

- Typical spacings: 8 to 20 feet
- Typical ratios of total arch heights to span: 1 to 4 and up to 1 to 8
- Typical span-to-depth ratio: 25

Wood Lamella Arches: 40- to 150-Foot Spans

- Typical ratios of arch heights to span: 1 to 4 and up to 1 to 6

How to Prevent Arbitrary Late-Arrival Design Changes

"The quality of a design is inversely proportional to the number of times it is improved. The inverse proportion doubles with each new participant."

—Murphy

How can you prevent excessive last-minute design changes from clients? Midstream revisions are costly and demoralizing to staff, and they throw schedules and budgets to the winds.

Here are some preventatives for the problem, offered by several skilled designers:

- Doug Hayes, a west coast solar home designer, programs all design decisions in advance. He leaves little opportunity for oversights and last-minute flashes. His central tool is an extensive "dream list" created during a client interview. He covers everything a client might possibly be concerned with—from ceiling heights to finishes to furnishings—before he draws a line. All items are systematically rechecked through design development. By the time production drawings are under way, virtually everything has been decided and confirmed. Late changes are few and incidental.

- Another, much larger, midwest firm also does a systematic, itemized, room-by-room walk-through with clients. Jerry Quebe of Hansen Lind Meyer (HLM) says: "The system catches those potential later embarrassments, such as finding out there's a light switch at the only spot we can put the filing cabinet." When HLM completes detailed room layouts, they have the users formally approve them. This checkout, combined with early-on systematic programming, assures that the drawings are basi-

57

cally ready to build from at the close of design development. This allows HLM direct reuse of design drawings as working drawings. Working drawings are off to a flying start, with 20 percent of the work already completed at the outset of the production phase. And by that time, later changes of mind by the client are few and far between.

• Lee Ward, a California designer, has a special device that inhibits clients from making arbitrary late changes. It's a simple PERT or CPM diagram of the design and production phases of the project showing time and cost estimates as originally agreed to with the client. A copy of the diagram is presented as part of the design service contract. A client who requests design changes after final design approval has to review the job diagram with the designer and participate in revising the time and cost budget. This makes the time and cost consequences of design revisions completely clear to the client—a strong inhibitor of capricious mind changes.

• A small-office design firm in Virginia uses a "big-office" technique that reportedly keeps changes, costs, and fees in line with reality. The tool is a checklist, a short-form version of the American Institute of Architects (AIA) Scope of Services list. Whenever a client asks for design services that have not been contracted for, or for extended services after designs have been approved, out comes the scope list and a calculator. The client is given a quick preview of the time and cost consequences of design revisions and, as in the previous example, has ample incentive for restraint.

• Sophisticated "systems drafting" offices report they beat the design revision problem at both ends. At the front end, composite assembly and overlay techniques make it possible to explore all reasonable design options in minimal time. Instead of drawing and redrawing variations and options, they physically move drawing components around on overlay pasteup sheets. Since pasteups are far easier to revise than drawings, it's possible to do exhaustive design studies before it's time to move on to production drawings. When doing design presentations, they have all the "decided" or fixed data on base sheets and the variable design possibilities on transparent overlays. That way it's possible to show a lot of options to help the client see all possibilities early on while spending comparatively little extra time on drawing. Since the base sheets are uncluttered with titles, rendering entourage, color, etc., they are available for continuation and direct reuse as working-drawing sheets.

The Planner's Lexicon, or How to Eschew Obfuscation

"Anything is possible as long as you don't understand what you are talking about."

—Murphy

Since words themselves are a problem-solving tool, it's important to understand the jargon of the design and planning profession. These definitions will get you through any university design studio critique, several Connecticut cocktail parties, and even through the awards issue of *Progressive Architecture.*

Archetypes.   This really means the first of a type, but designers use it mostly just to mean "type" because it sounds so much better.

Architectronic.   Architectural. In some circles, this is the only way to say "architectural." This is an all-purpose obfuscator that can be used in combination with every other word in this lexicon.

Becoming, the Process of.   This means growing or changing, but it is never to be used to explain what it is, precisely, that something is growing or changing into.

Biosphere.   Where things live. Always "threatened."

Design Constraint.   The reason you didn't design something as well as you would have otherwise. Always something you "work within."

Ecosphere.   Same as **biosphere.** Always "fragile."

Iconic.   Something that's the same as before. The contemporary way to say "traditional."

Impact. In planning, circumstances don't affect people, they "impact them." Say aloud to yourself a few times: "The modality might impact them adversely." Now you've got it.

Infrastructure. A structure beneath a structure. Similar to substructure, but not to be confused with substructure, structure, or superstructure. Always "disintegrating."

Modality. An attribute that impacts.

Mode. What something is doing. If your car is rolling down a hill, it is in the "rolling mode." When it crashes, it is in the "crashed mode."

Paradigm. The dictionary says paradigm is a pattern, example, or model. Among planners the word is considered an especially nice way to refer to sudden and radical change—change so radical and sudden that it wouldn't do just to call it a "radical change."

Parameter. A major quantifiable characteristic of a system. A parameter of your trip to a bar is distance. A parameter of success is whom you leave with. Two is usually plenty.

Pastiche. Architectural salad.

Place. A piece of property. The theme of numerous doctorates, papers, and design conferences as in:

    Ontology of Place. The qualities that a piece of property has.

    The Sense of Place. Perceiving a piece of property. Some places are referred to as not having a "sense of place," such as Oakland, California. But even Oakland has ontology.

Postmodernism. New buildings that look old, but are really just kidding.

Semiology. The word refers to signs and symbols. It has been widely used by designers and planners in recent years to refer to no discernible thing whatsoever. Feel free to use it in any context or application—preferably in reference to something like the "semiotics of place."

Sociogram. A chart that shows that most people like to be around people who are attractive and pleasant and don't like to be near people who are not. Best of all, it shows who's who in the ratings. Such charts gain the greatest return on investment when casually left lying around the office coffee break room.

Statement. That which a design makes. Always, always, always "bold."

Taxonomy. A list of everything you can think of about something. In lieu of actually starting work on a project you can do a taxonomy until the "parameters of the problem" are changed. Then you can do another taxonomy.

Topology. Surface. You can use this term in reference to things that don't even have a surface, such as the "topological semiotic of place," and nobody will challenge you on it.

chapter 4

Creative Shortcuts

"Take your problem and divide it into smaller and smaller and smaller pieces until it has disappeared."

—*Murphy's Recipe*

The scientific study of thinking and creative processes is a relatively new field. Most of what has been learned on the subject has been discovered in the past 20 years. The findings include some surprises. For example, most people evidently possess the same intellectual and creative capacities as professional innovators; the only detectable differences between creative and noncreative people are in educational experiences, attitude, personal ambition, and the use of specialized techniques.

New light has been cast on the nature of thinking processes. An immense variety of mental processes are popularly lumped together as "thinking." Thinking, in the problem-solving sense, is a singular mental process of goal-directed question asking, evaluation of answers, and further questioning. Professional problem solvers have learned methods of maintaining and controlling this process and for avoiding the diversions of "nonthought" mental processes. (Diversions include emotionalizing, reminiscing, random fantasizing, repetition of stock phrases, etc.) Professionals have also learned to maintain question-asking sequences subconsciously as well as consciously—a process that has its own peculiar rules.

The purpose of asking oneself questions in creative problem solving hasn't always been fully appreciated. Many thinkers have presumed that creative mental activity is ultimately beyond understanding, that ideas may or may not pop up from some mysterious realm, no matter what one might try to do about it. In actuality, creative problem solving turns out to be a simple scanning process. Any problem incorporates some unperceived things, actions, or attributes (or some combination of these) that are required to fulfill some stated need. Questions are feelers that help direct scanning toward the relatively few things, actions, or attributes that will provide elements of a solution.

If creative problem-solving processes are that simple—and if everyone has the capacity—why is creativity so rare? Many experts have asked the same question and have uncovered a number of factors that tend to inhibit or distort creative efforts.

Self-doubt is a major inhibitor. Painful childhood experiences with abortive creative efforts lead many people to accept the judgment that "some people have it and some don't." This judgment is fortified by popular educational notions which evaluate some children as "gifted" and others as not. (This notion is self-fulfilling and self-perpetuating. Years of experiments show that children who are expected by their teachers to be "gifted," "underachievers," or "retarded" will become so, regardless of their previous expressed talents.)

Education contributes to self-doubt in another way. Several educators have noted that creative problem solving, like any skill, requires theoretical knowledge and practice. Most schools provide neither of these. Students are left to learn creative thinking techniques strictly on their own, and many cultural factors combine to discourage the effort. For one thing, the steps toward finding solutions usually include formation, expression, and exploration of totally useless half-baked ideas. For those who are unaware that this is a normal and necessary part of creative activity—just a step along the way—this phase seems like a crazy dead end and proof of creative inadequacy either in themselves or in others.

This chapter deals with simple techniques that help overcome self-imposed barriers to creative functioning. It describes:

- Methods of comparing problems with analogous situations that may provide ready-made answers
- Question-asking sequences that help eliminate prejudgments, self-limiting viewpoints, and errors in comprehension of a problem

- Ways of increasing the variety of alternative approaches and choices of solutions

Practice is required with any of these techniques before they'll be reliably effective. The main rule in such practice, according to several authorities, is: Treat the problem-solving effort lightly; avoid any self-criticism over the unimaginative or poor ideas that inevitably occur. And one expert provides this warning: Some poor ideas will seem great at first glance, ideas that seem most exciting should be left to sit for a while before they are put into action.

Here are some effective "quicky" methods of problem solving. Besides being practical tools in themselves, they demonstrate important principles behind seemingly more mysterious problem-solving methodologies.

CREATIVE SHORTCUT ONE—REWORDING THE PROBLEM

Some problems remain unsolved solely because of an ambiguity or contradiction in terminology. Instant solutions appear when such problems are rephrased. Observation of such instances has resulted in the discovery of several useful rephrasing techniques.

In one method you first phrase the problem in a brief but complete statement. Then you replace each word of the problem statement, one by one, with new but related words. Sometimes only a few complete rewordings will clarify the problem sufficiently so that its solution becomes apparent.

In one example, a small conflict arose in the planning of an elementary school. The nurse's office had to be in the administrative suite, administration had to be near the street, and because of site peculiarities, the playground had to be a backyard for the building at one floor level below the administrative level. The problem: excessive distance, plus a flight of stairs, separated the nurse from the playground, where most major and minor student injuries occur. The problem could have been written off as just another unresolvable plan conflict, but the architect had strong personal reasons for concern over student safety.

The problem remained unresolved through early stages of planning. Finally, an associate familiar with the rewording system was asked for suggestions. He asked the architect for a verbal statement of the problem. The architect said: "How can we get the nurse's office both in the administrative suite and near the playground at the same time?"

The statement was written down and wording was changed through several restatements, such as: "How to move the medical room toward the street and yard simultaneously?" After a few minutes of such rewording, the solution became clear. The final rewording started with: "The first aid station. . . ." The "first aid" aspect hadn't been considered before. A station could be fitted within the playground storage room and equipped with cot, sink, and supplies at minimal cost. In case of injuries the nurse could be called down by the playground supervisor by intercom.

Another version of this method helps to channel thinking away from mistaken or misleading assumptions that may misdirect the solution search. This entails reversing evaluations and relationships of elements in the problem statement.

The architect just cited was trapped by an implicit assumption that injured children would have to be taken upstairs and far through the building before they could receive attention. If he had reversed this possibility and envisioned the nurse coming instead to the children, he might have reached the same solution provided by the problem-rewording system.

CREATIVE SHORTCUT TWO—QUESTIONING THE PROBLEM

Erroneous assumptions not only may block quick solving of problems, they may create problems where none exist. Many problems are unraveled quickly by some questioning in the form of inverted problem statements.

Instead of asking: "How can we solve this?" we might more appropriately ask: "Should we be doing this at all?" "Is this really a problem?" "Does the problem exist?" "If it does exist, is it really a problem or an opportunity?"

One way of making these questions more productive is to phrase them as declarations rather than as questions and to examine their possible truth. Try saying, for example: "We shouldn't be doing this because. . . ." Then reasons can be examined to justify that remark. It very often happens that excellent reasons come to light for not doing anything.

In one case an engineer informed his architect that the newest edition of the building code governing an out-of-state project showed a minimum live load requirement that was double their original assumption. They went ahead and "solved the problem" by redoing computations and resizing structural members. Everyone concerned thought that the new load requirement was unreasonable, but no one thought to question the authorities responsible for the new code. As it turned out, the new load requirement was as unreasonable as it seemed to be. It was a typographical error that slipped through a new edition of the code.

Drafters have drawn countless details to cover nonexistent conditions. Designers have laid out building plans for lots that couldn't legally support any building at all. More than a few projects have been abandoned after thousands of dollars worth of drawing when belated feasibility studies showed they would be hopeless money losers. These are all examples of work done on problems that either were not really problems or were the wrong problems.

If a problem definitely exists, and if action should be taken on it, it pays to review whether the problem might not contain some important advantage. An outstanding (and outlandish) example occurred during construction of a tribal peyote shrine at the Oklahoma City Cowboy Hall of Fame. The contractor called the architect with alarm when excavators hit a gushing spring right at the all-important center of the shrine. The architect called the client to warn of extra costs involved with capping the spring. The client, an Indian chief who also happened to be a real estate broker and a member of the "turn lemons into lemonade" school of thought, said: "No problem. We'll put in a wishing well instead of the peyote slab. Probably double our revenues."

CREATIVE SHORTCUT THREE—ENRICHING THE PROBLEM STATEMENT

As seen in previous examples, a view or statement of a problem can be either misleading or helpful in directing a solution search.

A productive view or statement of a problem is one that suggests a maximum number of analogies between attributes of the problem and other things that may contain solutions.

When listing attributes, look for one that seems especially important to the problem and ask: "What is this like?" A listing of likenesses—the more surrealistic the better—will usually open up fresh new viewpoints.

For example, an architect was designing a motor home for himself and his family. His initial schemes were all adequate, all "worked," but none were exciting. He decided to change his approach: "I sat down and started making a list of things about me and my family. I asked myself: 'What are we like when we're out traveling?' I listed things like 'driving through a giant museum,' and 'we're like giant, mobile eyeballs.' The kids were 'caged animals.'"

The analogies led the designer to minimize standard motor home furnishings and open up the floor plan and exterior walls to maximize views and play space. Special bin storage was devised for the fruits of roadside scavenging. Provision was made for skyports, camera obscura, telescope, microscope, and infrared and ultraviolet lamps for nighttime nature viewing. The designer expressed great satisfaction at meeting the problem in a new way. Now he and his family would have a sense-heightening tool for actively exploring the environment instead of just having a refuge on wheels.

The "what is it like?" system reportedly works best when applied freely and fancifully. It was the surrealistic "giant eyeball" analogy that directed the designer's thinking toward his family's most important needs and away from narrow focus on a "practical" floor plan.

CREATIVE SHORTCUT FOUR—ESSENCE DEFINITION

This method has been successfully applied in conceptualizing new building designs. The method consists of finding and stating the dominant intended activity within a proposed building. Actions and persons involved may be diverse, but normally one essential activity can be found which determines most of the other activities. Once this is found, it may suggest the best orientation for subsequent planning. Louis Kahn was a persuasive advocate of the concept, and he elaborated on it in many of his writings.

One medium-sized hospital was saved from becoming a typically unpleasant institution when the designer put aside his concentration of the stated needs of the hospital administration. He defined the essence of activity in the building as "people healing." This definition put the needs of patients, staff, doctors, and administrators in proper order of importance.

Rooms were designed so that patients could see out the windows from their beds (a rare provision up to that time). He created a strong ornamental scheme to reduce visual monotony. Courtyards, self-service snack bars, and other conveniences were added (after some argument with the clients) for ambulatory patients. Maternity patients were given direct access to their babies with "roll through" baby bin slots between patient rooms and the baby ward. Carpet flooring was specified. Ceilings, the main "view" for most patients, were decorated to the hilt with super graphics.

The net result of this patient-oriented design effort, as reported by the hospital administration: a patient recovery and turnover rate 15 percent above normal. The project became a notable architectural, medical, and financial success for all concerned. (Note: Since this example was first recorded in the 1960s, the amenities described have become reasonably common in hospital design. But people had to fight for the change.)

A variation on essence definition, called "negative essence definition," has also been applied to building planning. Here, the most unpleasant feature of typical buildings of the type being designed is defined, and that becomes the focal point of the problem statement.

The method was used in preliminary planning of an urban medical clinic. After a few visits to existing clinics, the negative essence definition came out loud and clear. The dominant activity in such clinics was "people waiting."

Most disturbing in the existing clinics was the problem of distracted mothers trying to control and entertain their miserably bored children. The waiting, in this project, couldn't be eliminated, but it was greatly ameliorated by the introduction of a small, indoor court playground with crawl-through mazes and other small-scale diversions.

This group of creative shortcuts demonstrates general principles that are found in all creative problem-solving processes. Chapter 5 describes problem-solving systems that apply those principles in more methodical fashion to meet specialized needs.

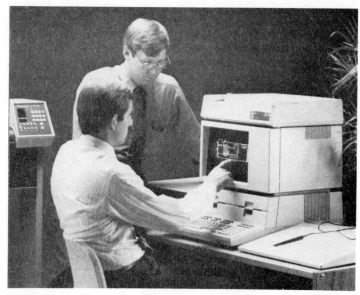

Figure 4.1   The computer is our finest problem-solving tool now, and by the mid 1980s most verbal and conceptual problem-solving systems such as those described in Chapters 4 and 5 will be available in the form of interactive software. Then, when that software is hooked into graphic systems, we'll be able to input complex problems verbally and receive options for solutions as either text, spoken word, numbers, or drawings or models. (Courtesy of Carrier.)

Attribute Listing, or What to Do When You Don't Know What to Do

When you don't know what you're doing:
  (a) Delegate it.
  (b) Do it neatly.
  (c) Make a list.
                    —Murphy's Multiple Choice Quiz

Here are three axioms that point to ways to keep any problem-solving session from bogging down:

1. A problem requires some change or changes to effect a solution.

2. There are a limited number of kinds of things that can be changed. These include parts, materials, locations, sizes, shapes, actions, sequences of action, functions, relationships, environment, movement, position (such as vertical). Although they can be subdivided further, these 12 are the basics.

3. There are a limited number of ways in which things can be changed. These include reversal, inversion, relocation, substitution, elimination, separation, transposition.

Whenever an idea-generating session grinds to a halt, new ideas can be sparked by slowly reviewing a list of qualities that pertain to the problem situation and comparing the list with a list of possible changes. This technique always reveals potential new ideas and gets extended creative thought processes flowing again.

Some specific case study examples of how this works and the ideas that can be generated were shown in Chapter 4 on creative shortcuts. As noted, reversal is a particularly rewarding approach because so many problem situations contain elements which are opposite in some way to what they should be. Just doing something the opposite way from the way you'd expect it to be done solves more problems than any other problem-solving technique in existence.

Another of the more effective idea stimulators is "combination." Virtually all inventions are born of some new combination of items in the foregoing lists.

Variations on the idea-generating checklist were used for years by well-known marketing men George Abrams and Alex Osborn. The Osborn list is "magnify, minify, rearrange, alter, adapt, modify, substitute, reverse, combine." The Abrams list includes many of the same items and adds idea prodders such as "association," "other uses," and "other forms."

Apparently neither Osborn nor Abrams knew precisely why their lists worked; they just knew they got results. The rules listed at the outset explain it. If you list the things and qualities involved in a problem situation and list all the kinds of changes that can be made, you can't help but find possible solutions somewhere in the mix and match of listed items. The listing system takes a little practice in order to get the hang of it, but it's probably the most effective fast-track problem-solving methodology you'll find anywhere.

Now here's a shortcut for the shortcut. If you're too pressured or impatient to methodically list and compare attributes and attribute changes, you can still find fresh ideas by making simple restatements of the problem situation.

As we saw in Chapter 4, the first step is to state the problem clearly in one sentence. Get the statement clearly and firmly in mind. Then start changing the words of the sentence, one by one, and rephrase the statement in as many ways as you can think of.

Multiple restatements of a problem help you avoid getting bogged down in dead-end mental ruts. Most people have experienced a flash of an idea after wrestling with a problem because they suddenly see the problem in a whole new way. "Reseeing," or throwing new light on a problem, usually occurs just because the problem is restated or suddenly understood in new and different terms.

Practical Problem-Solving Techniques

"Complex problems always have simple, easy-to-understand wrong answers."

—Murphy

This chapter describes three effective professional-level problem-solving methods. Any of them, conscientiously learned and applied, will expedite problem-solving meetings and will help solve most any creative or technical problem you might encounter.

BRAINSTORMING

"Brainstorming"[1] is the most widely known creative "group think" system. It is also widely misunderstood. Amateurish misuse of the system is rampant, especially in architects' troubleshooting conferences.

Though brainstorming has been misunderstood and misused, it

---

[1] Invented by Alex F. Osborn, author of *Applied Imagination*, Scribner, New York, 1953.

has generated thousands of practical ideas for business, science, and industry. The successes come most readily when certain simple procedural rules are observed.

In a typical brainstorm session, a group leader states the problem and asks participants to start shooting out suggestions. The suggestions may be totally wild and impractical. This is good. The object of the session is not to get immediate answers, but to find fruitful hints and leads toward answers. It is the group leader's responsibility to encourage imaginativeness by being far out in his or her own suggestions. He or she must never trample on someone else's ideas and must firmly block others from doing so. If a participant expresses criticism or ridicule, the group leader should signal the offender to stop.

The group leader or another participant can record the ideas as they come up by listing key words that will call forth the ideas later. Detailed notes are unnecessary. Often the best solution doesn't appear until after the meeting, when the list of ideas is reviewed.

Brainstorming is a simple procedure, it's enjoyable for most participants, and it can be amazingly productive. It works well for two reasons: It reduces the fear of failure (since there are no "wrong" suggestions); this fear is—as noted previously—the foremost inhibitor of creativity. Second, the participants' minds are opened to a wide range of directions that otherwise would come to mind only sporadically over a long period of hard thinking and subconscious incubating.

Architects and engineers have a lot of difficulty using the system or sticking to its rules. One common attitude is that brainstorming is a kind of "creativity by committee" that smothers the individual in regimentation and compromise within the group. In actuality, the group is there to stimulate rather than repress individual creativity; each idea suggests other ideas. (Brainstorming can be applied individually and privately as well as in group settings, but group meetings are considered most profitable.)

Some architects and engineers find they cannot tolerate the almost insane expressions that come up when an idea is still in a formative stage. They have been trained, after all, to be clear-eyed and critical. They find it impossible to sit by patiently and listen to babbling about lasers or electromagnetic fields when there is a serious problem to be dealt with. Needless to say, it is pointless to require people with rigid personalities to participate in brainstorming sessions.

PROBLEM-SOLVING TECHNIQUES—SYNECTICS

"Synectics" has been described as a sort of "superbrainstorming." Like brainstorming, it is designed for group use, but it can be applied privately by individuals. It is not considered especially economical for dealing with routine problems; users say it works best with the worst sticklers and is especially effective when applied to design problems, inventions, and, to a large degree, troubleshooting.

A synectics session generates and accelerates subconscious solution searches that characterize normal creative thinking. Diverse chains of thought, odd similes, analogies, and relationships are sought out through mental "excursions." Excursions can take several forms. One excursion sequence might go like this:

1. The problem is stated and explained.

2. The attributes of objects connected with the problem are examined and analyzed. (An expert on the subject of the problem may be sitting in to provide technical data and evaluate final results.)

3. Off-the-cuff solutions are aired out. This is called the "purge."

4. If no clear-cut solutions come out of the "purge," some desirable related goals are added to the original problem.

5. One auxiliary goal is selected, and the session departs wholly from consideration of the original problem. Analogies to the auxiliary goal are sought from randomly selected and unrelated fields such as the "world of bridges," "movies"—whatever.

6. If an item comes to mind regarding some aspect of the unrelated field that relates strongly to the auxiliary goal or to the problem at hand, it is examined further and possibly fitted to the problem.

Throughout most of the synectics session, the original problem is deliberately forgotten. Experience has shown that this aids in passing over narrow, obvious, and unproductive channels of thinking. Naturally, the original problem leaps back to consciousness as soon as a prospective solution is touched upon in the random stages of the "excursion."

Synectics has produced many remarkable technical inventions, ingenious solutions to management problems, and some promising architectural concepts.

• The problem of planning a small architectural office was recently treated to an "excursion," with quite unexpected results. The problem was stated as: "We need a small drafting room that will reduce waste motion and hunting-around time to a minimum." An auxiliary goal was defined: "Remove the clutter of shelves, files, plan drawers, etc." (The reader can consider his or her own normal approaches to such a problem and compare personal procedures with the highlights of the "excursion.")

After some "purge" solutions were suggested and set aside, the discussion focused on examples of clean and efficient activity in areas unrelated to the problem. One example—that of the centrifugal pump—came up and was passed over. Later someone mentioned merry-go-rounds in an entirely different connection. A unique solution came into focus almost immediately.

The solution: a central piece of furniture, octagonal in plan, with several revolving layers of storage spaces—like lazy-susan layer-cake shelves. Drafting tables would be satellite arms of the octagon. All technical literature, books, supplies, files, sketches, etc., would be stored within the layered compartments. Any drafter would have access to stored materials by revolving the appropriate layer of compartments around to his or her station. The top surface of the unit would be fixed as space for reference drawing and check prints. This seemed to knock off both problems of walk-around time and office clutter in one blow, and it was achieved by abandoning the "real" situation and imagining analogies that were far afield from the image of a drafting studio.

Here are a couple of other practical products of architectural synectics sessions:

- A vacation home that can physically expand and contract according to occupancy and be readily closed up and sealed against intruders and vandals during nonuse.
- A "wheel spoke" suburban library building plan that provides almost instant book access for users and reduces staff problems of supervision and stack maintenance. (This scheme was later used in bookstore planning nationally.)

PROBLEM-SOLVING TECHNIQUES— VALUE ENGINEERING

Value Engineering (VE) is a specialized thinking technique that is exclusively applied to problems of value and cost. Its successes are measured in dollars and cents, and, for the corporations and government agencies that use the system, these successes have mounted into the millions.

The point of such scrutiny is not merely to "build cheaply." The purpose is to build as well as, or better than, usual *and* cheaply. Every product, material, and work procedure in existence can be improved, and most people have had the experience of finding such improvements. Most such experiences are accidental and rare; Value Engineering seeks to make the experience deliberate and controlled.

An architectural Value Engineering session usually starts with a preliminary building design. A step-by-step sequence of analysis is applied to each element of the design. First, an element is identified by name, and its function is defined in two words. The two-word functional definition of a large window might be "provides view." The cost of the item is noted. The item is checked for auxiliary functions. In the case of the window, the auxiliary function might be defined as "provides ventilation." The cost of the auxiliary function is noted. Then the questioning begins:

1. What part provides the primary function?
2. What part or parts provide the auxiliary functions?
3. Are these functions necessary?
4. Can these functions be provided by something else? What?
5. What would something else cost?

A southern California designer and builder of contemporary homes, anxious to cut costs without lowering his high, prize-winning design standards, applied this process. He found dozens of improvements within a single afternoon of analysis. As an example, his window walls had previously included integrated operable fenestration for ventilation. The VE breakdown showed that the ventilation function could be provided by hinged transoms between exposed ceiling beams. The large glass areas could be fixed within simple wood frames, and the operable windows could be dispensed with entirely—at substantial savings per dwelling unit.

VE has been applied on thousands of occasions to reduce building costs in design phases, and, less fortunately, during redesign phases after bids come in over budget. It has to be considered an essential part of design management.

Formal Value Engineering techniques have been in development since World War II. Value Engineering is now an established profession, represented by a national organization, the Society of American Value Engineers. Check your library information service for the current national or regional society locations.

There is a wealth of creative and troubleshooting methodologies for the design manager: Delphi, morphological thinking, Kepner-Tregoe, idea tracking, lateral thinking, Bobele-Buchanan, and several others. One of the most comprehensive studies of all the leading methodologies is *Techniques of Structured Problem Solving*, by Arthur B. Van Gundy, Jr., published by Van Nostrand, New York, 1981.

Chopping with a Finer Blade— Occam's Razor

"When you encounter inexplicable behavior, ask: What is the payoff, and who is the beneficiary?"

—Murphy the Elder

William of Occam was a fourteenth-century philosopher. His colleagues were hopelessly entangled in all manner of convoluted arguments and off-the-wall hypotheses about the nature and meaning of reality. Occam proposed a test, a way of cutting through the verbal clutter.

Occam proposed that if you want to understand a situation, chances are that the simplest and most obvious explanation is the correct one. Or, to put it another way: "Don't invent any more hypotheses than are necessary."

Many souls spend much of their lives concocting complicated explanations to account for life's events. On the personal level, for example, many people invent the most elaborate notions to explain why other people aren't behaving in a desired fashion—why the spouse isn't affectionate, why the kids aren't obedient, and why friends and coworkers aren't supportive. The most likely real reason is the simplest one: They have no particular reason to be.

In design management virtually any complex explanation could profitably be replaced with something simpler. For example, the officers of a large architectural and engineering firm were ready to trash their design director because he didn't come up with a winning proposal for an important airport job. Everything appeared to be in their favor—experience, dedication, the right consulting team—the only variable seemed to be their approach to the design itself. The rejection didn't make sense. A simple explanation would have been that the proposal was fine but the county commissioners responsible for the airport project were promised kickbacks by the winning firm, which indeed was the case.

Environmental Design Failures

This chapter names the most common hazards and failures in
building design: errors in building siting, heating and cooling
failures, lighting problems, noise, safety hazards, and materials
failures. If you remember these particular problems, you can
avoid most of the ills that plague over half of all building owners.

SITE CLIMATE

The dangers of overlooking regional and site microclimates were
vividly illustrated several years ago in a western state. A tract of
architect-designed, semiluxury homes was erected along the
northeast slopes of a picturesque canyon. The homes were bought
up quickly, but the new owners soon began having second
thoughts. For one thing, their fireplace flues wouldn't function
because of downdrafts and wind eddies along the hill slopes.
Their homes were built on pole-supported platforms, over what

turned out to be a wind channel; this meant cold floors and unusually high heat loss due to air infiltration and leakage.

Some owners sold out. Some initiated costly corrective measures to alleviate the nuisances. Nuisance turned to disaster when hard-driving, yearly desert winds came along. As winds roared over the hills, they accelerated to hurricane velocities by a venturi effect of the splayed canyon site. Buildings and their supports were raised upward by 100-mile per hour gusts; several homes tore loose and collapsed on the hill slopes. The architect won the lawsuits that ensued because the court held the superhigh canyon winds were not reasonably predictable, but despite winning he still had to abandon his practice.

In another case, prevailing wind (and solar orientation) was ignored in the planning of a west coast landmark office tower and pedestrian plaza. The shaded plaza is located along a city street well known as a wind channel. The plaza was originally equipped with a fountain that effectively drenched passersby during wind gusts. The fountain is now permanently unused, as is the plaza.

Light winds become a problem when they are compressed through shallow malls. One eastern high-rise was designed with a large, interior, ground floor court, which was open at opposite ends. Prevailing breezes accelerate to small gale velocities within this space and virtually block access to the building.

Similar environmental mishaps have been reported across the country:

- An enormous housing project in a cool climate with an extensively planted plaza—neither the planting nor the occupants can survive the perennial shade cast by the high-rise.
- A civic center entry and plaza enclosed within an L-shaped building plan that is oriented toward the wind in such a way that it generates endless dust- and trash-laden whirlwinds within the plaza. Most users of the building now use an inconvenient, but windless, remote side entrance.

Other site climate factors that can affect building and site use include fog belts, frost pockets, and rainy slopes. Such conditions often vary markedly over just a few yards of distance. Ground water, which is particularly variable from place to place, has had severe effects on some smaller buildings. Crawl space buildings are often built on wet land, but with only nominal code-required crawl space ventilation; ground water evaporation under such buildings can be nearly as great as evaporation from an open pond of water—with markedly musty effects on interior building climate.

Why do such problems get through when it's so obviously easy or mandatory to investigate site conditions—especially in these days of environmental impact reports (EIRs)? Most often the EIRs are not read by designers. As often as not, sites are not even visited by designers, much less subjected to any thorough research and evaluation. There are obvious exceptions, as when the design firm and client make a strong commitment to energy conservation, or use of solar energy, or both. But in most cases, building design begins as a set of hypothetical sketches for a feasibility study, which lead to other studies for regulatory and financing agencies, which at some point end up as a real design for a real building. Since everything has been tentative from the start, there's no time or motivation for site analysis.

SITE AND SUN

The perils of ill-considered solar orientation were brought home to the architects of a new library building at a midwestern college. Their designer had provided for a large stretch of unshielded, 14-foot-high glass frontage across the southern face of the structure. This was designed to "catch maximum daylight." Complaints of sun glare and heat gain began coming in as soon as the building was opened to student use. In a complete misunderstanding of the problem, the client and designer agreed to add a new layer of glazing to create an insulating air space. Insulated air space helps reduce heat loss from a building in winter, to be sure, but is wholly ineffective in blocking direct radiant heat gain. The heat gain remained intolerable, and heavy draperies were installed as a further barrier. The drapes delayed heat absorption somewhat, but they created a hot air pocket which eventually radiated itself into the room each day so that use of the building in the afternoons was still impossible. The library maintenance staff then covered most of the glass with aluminum foil, which made the interior of the library unpleasantly dark. Later, when reflective translucent polyester film came on the market, that was installed to radiate heat while allowing in more light. That helped, but the resulting reflecting glare is a general visual irritant on the campus, and it forces instructors in the building across the way to close their blinds during late afternoons.

That design firm has also created elementary schools with large windows that are oriented in such a way that children "fry like eggs" each day, according to the school district's chief administrator.

Lee Ward, a California architect who has given special attention to sun and orientation problems for over 20 years, says: "Glass and sun are a brutal combination. . . . Architects use too much glass in the wrong orientation and then try to solve the problems they created with devices that either don't work or that contradict the reasons for having glass in the first place."

He lists these examples: Cantilevered sun shades, effective for blocking solar heat gain when properly designed for sun angles, are also sometimes expected to control glare from direct sunlight. This they cannot do at the worst glare times (morning and afternoon). Interior sunlight controls (such as blinds and shades) block direct-sun glare, but do little to prevent heat gain. Operable exterior louvers have been successfully used in some cases, but because they are expensive to maintain and easy to vandalize, they haven't become well-accepted. Multiple layers of exterior horizontal sunshades have been effective in blocking both heat and glare from the sky, but they can transmit unwanted reflected heat from neighboring pavement. In addition, since these block off large amounts of light and view, the question always arises: Why bother with the large window area in the first place?

SITE AND SOUND

Acoustics consultants have been called in by building owners to advise on problems of street noise, neighboring mechanical equipment, and echoing alleyways and courtyards. These are all considered obvious potential noise problems that could have been discovered through architects' site investigations. Some owners are keenly aware of this and are vocal in their resentment of apparent architect carelessness.

Popular home builders magazines occasionally print some "architectural guidance" in blocking out street and neighbor noise. They suggest planting "trees, vines, and shrubs." This traditional advice is considered misleading by acoustical engineers, who point out that, at most, only a few decibels can be attenuated by even dense, extensive planting. Distance and mass are noted as the best noise barriers. If sensitive building areas can't be located away from outside noise sources, sound insulating construction or high masonry barriers may do the job. Another possible solution: It's sometimes possible to successfully mask distracting bursts of exterior noise with the steady noise of fountains or controlled diffuser hum within the building.

OVERSIGHTS IN INTERIOR
CLIMATE CONTROL

Considering that the costs of a building's mechanical system may constitute up to as much as 40 percent of total construction cost, it makes sense to start planning the system right along with the rest of the design. There is ample evidence that major problems with mechanical systems are born in the initial conceptualization of buildings. In addition, much of the equipment put in a building to provide for human comfort actually violates or interferes with that comfort. Some typical examples follow.

- *Outside air intakes* are often located as a second thought to meet some need in mechanical room planning. They sometimes appear at the hottest side of a building, at sun-baked pavements, and even face-to-face with the exhaust of adjacent buildings. (One architect was shocked to discover that his staff had permitted installation of an intake near the driveway entrance to a parking garage. Waiting cars sat idling and spewed their exhausts into the building's air-conditioning system.)

- *Air returns and supply* are sometimes planned without regard for room uses. Lounges, dining rooms, and other gathering places are subject to smoky inversion layers when air returns are not provided near the ceiling. Conversely, dust-producing rooms or entry areas in dusty regions are best served by returns near the floor.

  Some architects provide returns at the floor or wall base of large windows, with the intention of catching cooled air from the glass before it penetrates the rest of the space. But if warm air outlets are provided in the interior of the space, the warm air is ineffectual in warming the glass; the room air motion becomes opposite to that which is most desirable. The glass areas, allowed to remain cold, cause heat drain and are especially subject to severe condensation.

- *Large return and supply wall grilles* frequently turn up near office desks or other workstations, and, almost as often, they end up being covered with cardboard by the employees. Drafts have been found to be more than a climate problem. They can be a serious working nuisance, and, as maintenance personnel have observed, they can be taken as serious personal insults by building occupants.

  There's some disagreement about the maximum allowable air velocity from supply registers, but engineers advise that if people are likely to be within direct range of nearby registers, the air velocity should be kept under 100 feet per minute. Preferably, locations of all registers—especially air-conditioning supply—should be planned to avoid blowing any direct breeze on people.

A common residential source of drafts is the interior heating unit—or fireplace—which pulls cool air across living areas from exterior walls and windows. As noted previously, heating should be provided at each large window. Some architects avoid fireplace drafts by including a small extra outside air supply to the firebox.

• *Overload and inadequate controls* recently helped destroy the grand opening celebration of a new civic building. Ventilation design was based on nominal day-to-day occupancy; the system couldn't cope with a massive crowd of people. As far as most visitors were concerned, the building's air-conditioning was no good. Technical explanations about nominal loading or overloading did nothing to persuade citizens that the building was not misdesigned.

Periodic overloads in showrooms, civic meeting rooms, art galleries, conference rooms, etc., have all presented the same problem. Sometimes the problem is purely a matter of control. Potentially crowded spaces in larger buildings are often tied in with automatic controls governing large general zones of much lower average occupancy. If separate controls aren't feasible, it may be possible to include simple operable sash or plain outside mechanical ventilators to provide for the special overload occasions.

• *Floors, hot and cold,* have raised some unexpected problems. Some heating engineers report that floors heated to 80° or more will cause serious complaints. Some people, especially older persons, suffer strong discomfort and swelling of feet and ankles after several hours' contact with such flooring.

Some pilotis buildings—including those in warm climates—are reported to become refrigerators when outside temperatures drop. The cooled floors pull radiant heat directly from the bodies of occupants. Even if the air temperature is maintained at 75° and more, the radiant loss is enough to chill the occupants. In addition to the radiant loss, uniform room temperatures are said to be impossible to maintain, no matter how much heated air is pumped in. Extrathorough engineering attention to insulation is the only way to block environmental failures of raised construction.

Many mechanical engineers have commented that a large number of problems of mechanical cost, maintenance, efficiency, and noise are traceable to the common practice of planning mechanical systems as incidental to other aspects of the building. Here are some expert suggestions for avoiding such problems:

■ Common late-hour conflicts and revisions are avoided if the distribution system is decided simultaneously with structure and floor plan. Main ducts and branches should be located early and revised as plans are revised. Building design revisions made without reference to the mechanical system often create high unforeseen construction expenses, which mean excessively high bids and necessitate later backtracking and revision of the overall design.

- Try to provide a central location for the heating and air-conditioning plant. Establish this early in preliminary planning and work to make it stick. The central location will shorten supply runs and simplify engineering design, and if the engineer can be assured that equipment locations are fixed, his or her work can proceed more rapidly without fear of false starts.

- Locate fresh air intakes and exhaust early in the design stage. These are often left for late consideration and sometimes result in unsatisfactory last-minute alterations in the floor plan and exterior elevations.

LIGHTING PROBLEMS

Bad lighting is often so subtle that it won't raise outright complaints but will still affect behavior. Certain rooms become unused, people congregate in some parts of common spaces and not in others, employees in some work spaces take inordinate numbers of quick breaks just to get away from their rooms. If asked, most building occupants reacting to lighting problems will not be able to tell you why they prefer certain spaces over others. But if you get a few people together with clipboards and ask them to walk around and look specifically for lighting problems, they'll find plenty. And they'll find them in virtually any building you care to survey.

Here are some of the more common and severe sources of lighting problems:

- *Reliance on daylight* as a presumed economy, as a means of decreasing the need for artificial light, often backfires. Large glass areas at office and classroom spaces sometimes create such high brightness at the perimeters of these rooms that interior artificial light has to be increased to avoid excessive contrast. Similarly, skylighting in some rooms creates such apparent contrasting darkness at adjacent ceilings that the total effect is one of general dimness. The problem is worsened when the surfaces adjacent to the windows or skylights are especially dark.

Some architects have provided extensive skylighting in classrooms to compensate for bright window areas. And they have added ingenious ceiling screening systems for darkening rooms. In such cases, the teachers usually tire of fooling with the ceiling skylight blinds and keep them permanently closed.

The consensus of those who have striven to introduce lots of natural lighting is to use extreme care in design and not to count on any economies. The increased need for artificial lighting, the added maintenance, and the extra load on heating and cooling systems tend to turn natural light into a luxury item.

• *Floor glare* accompanies use of large glass walls adjacent to reflective flooring. The discomforting wash of light also reveals the inevitable irregularities and waviness of the surface. It is recommended that unshielded, full-height glazing not be used in combination with reflective flooring.

• *Ceiling fixture glare* is likely to be pronounced where fixtures are located below the ceiling line and no upward light is provided. A rule often emphasized by lighting experts is that glare is a function of brightness contrast—not brightness alone. Even a moderately bright light can be glary against a relatively dark background.

• *Veiling reflection*—unpleasant reflected glare on work surfaces or reading matter—is costly as well as unpleasant. Lighting experts estimate that a room with a 100-footcandle lighting level may provide the working visibility of a 25-footcandle room because of veiling reflections. Ceiling fixtures can be decreased in number and lighting quality improved by use of polarizing or other special lens fixtures that reduce downward light and increase lighting output laterally at 30° or so. (It is downward direct light, within a 40° cone, that produces most reflected glare.)

• *Day and night contrast* has become a serious problem as a result of the widespread use of high-brightness fluorescent lighting. The brightness is usually mitigated during the day by combination with incoming daylight. At night the dilution disappears, and previously unnoticed fixtures take on a much stronger presence. Some normally innocuous interiors are described as gruesome at night, especially upon first approach or entry from the dark outdoors. The extensive studio floor areas of an architecture school of a major university remain virtually unused after dark, partly because of this problem.

• *Design by ceiling pattern*—a traditional pastime of drafting staff assigned to do reflected ceiling plans—creates many inefficiencies and a few problems. Primarily, lights are placed for the sake of a pattern without regard for specific occupant needs. If occupant use of a room and furniture arrangement is predictable, it is recommended that fluorescent ceiling fixtures be set to run parallel to the occupants' line of sight. This cuts direct ceiling fixture glare. And side lighting is considered to be up to 50 percent more effective for most work activities.

Hallways—with much less area to be illuminated—are unpleasantly overlit in comparison with larger rooms when they have the same lighting pattern as the larger rooms.

• *Uniform room brightness,* the ideal that prevailed in the 1940s and 1950s, is still sought with uniformly unfortunate success. Uniformity—which results in minimal shadows—eliminates perception of texture and surface form. Occupants are left with blank, sterile, disorienting environments.

Owners of some"uniformly lit" buildings with nonstop wall-to-wall luminous ceilings have been forced to use clumsy corrective measures, such as disconnecting portions of the lighting or adding extra fixtures to create shadows.

• *Excessive dimness* has also occurred in some new projects where architects have overreacted to high-brightness contrasts or all-pervasive diffused lighting. An urban branch library was designed with incandescent downlights throughout, to help create a desired "warm, homelike" atmosphere. These worked fairly well over the reading tables. But the light failed to reveal book titles on the shelves. Library users had to remove volumes from the shelves and hold them upward toward their faces before titles became legible. Auxiliary shelf lamps had to be added as an expensive afterthought.

NOISE

Noise and Sound within Rooms

Some rooms are supposed to carry sound; some aren't. Too often both types receive identical acoustical treatment. Some results of indiscriminate use or nonuse of absorbent acoustical treatment are described in the next few pages.

• *Sound loss* is the usual complaint of users of conference spaces, lecture rooms, and small multipurpose auditoriums. The rooms are "nice and quiet," but speakers have to raise their voices and repeat themselves to get the sound across.

The problem is the result of excessive use of absorptive materials.

In extreme cases such rooms include carpeting, drapes, upholstery, and acoustical treatment across the ceiling and down some walls. These prevent sufficient reverberation (or "lingering") of sound within the space.

To convey wanted sound in lecture rooms, it is important to provide a hard, reflective surface behind the main speaker. Ceiling acoustical treatment belongs toward the rear of the room opposite the speaker area. Absorption is called for at the back wall of large lecture rooms to stop sound from bouncing back once it has been delivered. Since accessible acoustical tile will be picked to pieces by occupants, it is recommended that pegboard or other hard, perforated or slotted surface be applied over glass fiber or other absorptive material. (This rear wall treatment isn't normally required if the room doesn't exceed 40 feet in length.)

Sound loss in conference rooms can be avoided by keeping acoustical treatment limited to the perimeter of the ceiling. The ceiling over the conference table should be hard and reflective.

• *Excessive reverberation* may occur in areas where applied absorptive materials are sometimes considered unnecessary, as in public corridors and stairwells. This has been a real problem in school buildings. It creates an atmosphere of wholesale bedlam between class times.

Some concerned officials warn that chaotic reverberation could add to panic and become a menace during fires or other emergency evacuations. For general comfort and safety, some absorption in stairwells and exit corridors is strongly recommended.

• *Acoustical imbalance* is characteristic of churches because of varying acoustic needs and varying occupancies. Church reverberation is high when least appropriate: during small services, funerals, etc. (coughs, dropped keys, and other distractions seem magnified at such times). On the other hand, excess absorption occurs when least desirable—when the auditorium is filled by the sound-absorbing congregation. Worshippers—especially older persons—have to strain to hear. And music is deadened by the decreased reverberation.

One suitable solution is being urged by acoustics consultants who are willing to do battle with the church tradition of uncomfortable wood pews. The wood pews are highly reflective. When absorbent upholstery is used, the auditorium takes on the acoustical properties of full occupancy. This eliminates the problem of uncontrollable sound quality variation due to varying attendance. It also simplifies the problem of finding a compromise between the acoustical needs of sermon speech and sermon music.

Another kind of imbalance is found in multiuse rooms such as cafetoriums. Typically, such places are put to acoustically incompatible uses, such as dining, meetings, speeches, films, and plays and musical events. Some guides exist for minimizing the problems: long, rectangular rooms should be avoided; a separate space or enclosed, sound-treated cabinet is mandatory for film projectors; a backstage sounding board is essential for recitals and dramas.

Noise between Rooms

There is a basic misunderstanding about sound and noise that is virtually universal. It's the idea that surface acoustical treatments will stop sound from passing between rooms. Thus designers and building owners will cover rooms top to bottom with acoustical tile or other absorbent materials to protect neighboring rooms from sound transfer. The sound just flies right through it. These materials reduce the reflection of sound within the room, but they are not the barrier most people think they are.

This misunderstanding has been evident in a number of newer buildings where partitions stop at the ceiling line; the suspended acoustical ceilings have been expected to contain the room noises. Because of this problem, occupants of many buildings have found that they cannot use adjacent rooms simultaneously. Designers used acoustical tile suspended ceilings and provided no above-ceiling barriers. Until barriers were added later, at considerable extra cost, only every other room could be used at one time.

Some Related Room-to-Room Noise Problems

• *Partition sound transmission* is almost inevitably higher than architects are led to expect from published laboratory ratings. Lab ratings are usually summarized as averages for a wide range of sounds. Some partitions work well for blocking some frequencies and not others. In addition, lab-tested partitions are installed and sealed with optimal care, care that isn't normally given on a job site. Differences between laboratory and on-the-job installations can exist by as much as 40 percent in the overall transmission of sound.

Expectations of sound protection must be lowered to allow for differences between lab test conditions and the job site. If good sound protection is essential, special construction must be detailed, specified, and thoroughly inspected on the job.

Sound-insulating walls of wood frame construction are often detailed in the "staggered stud" pattern to block direct transfer of airborne sound. However, these walls are also often built on a single plate which connects the studs, therefore, and greatly reduces the intended sound attenuation.

• *Sound leaks* further diminish the value of partitioning. Some architects have reported that expensive wall systems selected for high sound-reduction value ratings seem to provide no noticeable reduction in comparison with cheaper systems. The reason is that sound propagates efficiently through small air passages and through adjacent structures or equipment. Tests show that a 1-inch-diameter hole in a 10-foot-square partition can increase total net sound transmission by 100 percent. It's obvious from this test what a few small gaps at the floor, ceiling, corners, and panel connectors can do to a partition's sound transmission rating.

Many other kinds of sound leaks are built into partitions. One such leak results from the drafting practice of drawing electrical wall outlets back-to-back on working-drawing floor plans. Even if wall thickness doesn't allow back-to-back installation, adjacent outlets serving opposite wall surfaces produce about the same sound leakage. Only one outlet should be installed within any one stud space.

Space around baseboard heaters or other continuous mechanical equipment below window perimeter should be filled in with a sound barrier at partition lines. Unsealed spaces allow intolerably large amounts of sound to pass between adjoining rooms.

Fireplaces provided for tenants in one well-known and very expensive apartment building are never used. The flues have now been clogged with newspapers and rags by the residents, who discovered that they were unintentionally sharing family intimacies with their neighbors, through the cross-connected flue system. This is an example of an ancient sound problem that still recurs, even in brand-new buildings.

Sound tube connections between rooms are also provided by ductwork—especially T branches of ducts that provide a cross traffic of sound. Such connections have been observed in such unfortunate locations as between restrooms, hospital rooms, lawyers' offices, and apartment dwellings.

• *Doors and windows* may be the weakest links in sound control. Louvered doors or doors cut off at the bottom for return air always pass sound freely. Some architects and designers believe sound will not run against the direction of air flow. In reality, air movement has little effect on the propagation of sound waves.

Cheap single-door connections between hotel and motel suites are still provided in some projects, with inevitably unsatisfactory results. Double doors or specially detailed, sound-sealed doors are a must to block major transmission of noise from room to room.

Adjacent and cross-facing doors along corridors are sometimes an unavoidable potential noise nuisance. If they can be more widely separated and staggered, some of the sound transfer can be reduced.

Operable windows next to partitions of adjacent apartments, offices, and classrooms may nullify most sound protection of the partitions. In many school buildings, when window hoppers are open, students seated near the rear of classrooms can hear the neighboring teacher better than their own. Adjacent operable windows should be avoided near these partition lines.

• *Partition-borne sound* is sometimes worse than leakage because of the magnifying effects of resonant partitions. Major complaints arise over wall-mounted televisions in hospitals and hotel or motel rooms. Wall-mounted telephone and intercom buzzers may be greatly amplified by a resonating partition surface. The best solution is simply to keep such noisemakers off the partitions. Where these and other noisy items, such as chalkboards or cabinets with slammable doors, must be on partitions, use gasketing generously to reduce the vibration transfer through the walls.

Building Noise

No one knows the full extent or costs of the noise generated by building equipment and appurtenances, but there are clues that the cost is enormous. In a University of California study of over 100 lecture rooms, for example, about one-third were considered unsatisfactory because of noise. Many were no longer used at all. Well over half of the unused rooms were plagued particularly by ductwork noise. Here's a summary of the usual equipment noise problems:

• *Fan room noise* has been an extreme nuisance where belts, motors, bearings, or other components are shoddy, badly installed, or ill-maintained. Even good equipment can generate noise, so some sound control should be considered if important rooms are served within a short distance from the fan room. Flexible joints at the main ducts in the fan room help block direct transmission through the duct material. Sound can also be attenuated some by use of one-half-inch or thicker glass fiber duct lining extending about 10 times the diameter of the main duct.

• *Air flow noise* occurs as air exceeds 900 feet per minute in the main ducts. Noise can be acute when air flow approaches 2000 to 3000 feet per minute, especially at sharp turns and branch connections. With increasing use of high-velocity systems, extra care is required to keep duct pathways away from important quiet spaces.

• *Diffuser noise* is considered desirable as a means of masking sporadic noise distractions and giving some cover for conversational privacy. To avoid extremes, it is recommended that air velocity at diffusers be kept below 400 to 500 feet per minute for registers with one-half-inch slots.

• *Mechanical room noise* may be broadcast to other areas despite springs, rubber mountings, and other isolation devices. Rigid plumbing pipe or electrical conduit connections will short-circuit isolation devices and transmit sound throughout the structure. Heavy vibrating equipment is sometimes located at the center of upper-floor bays or spans. This has created severely disturbing low-frequency vibration noise throughout all levels of lighter-frame buildings.

• *Elevators* have been a problem in a few high-rise residential buildings where living areas adjoin the hoistways. Although most modern equipment is smooth and silent, the movement of the cab can create disturbing "woofs" because of sudden squeezes and releases of air against projecting sills and beams. Flush wall construction for the shafts is desirable. If there is more than one hoistway, air pressure can be relieved by providing large openings between hoistways in the lowest basement walls.

COORDINATION PROBLEMS

These problems were noted in a tour of a new retail center:

• Conduit that had been bent upward from the floor slab to feed electrical outlets at columns poked out at the column base. The columns had inadequate furring to compensate for the conduit bending radius.

• Partitions that were supposed to extend through the ceiling to the upper-floor slab were stopped short by a maze of horizontal piping.

• Conduits that had been placed in an upper-floor slab and turned down to feed ceiling fixtures created barriers to the ductwork that followed. Some ductwork was then cut to fit around the conduits as well as around some water supply and soil pipes.

• The central mechanical plant floor was covered with water. Although equipment leakage and condensation was nominal, the architect and consultants had failed to get together on the need for generous floor slopes and drains.

• Several plumbing cleanouts and steam line valves were absolutely inaccessible after intervening equipment was installed.

- One ceiling hatch was blocked by a low-hanging mixing box and could be opened only about 6 inches.

- Doors to the electric closet and switchboard room had to be replaced with louvered doors to provide ventilation. The heat buildup common to such equipment had been overlooked.

- Foundation wall sleeves that were installed according to the architectural drawings didn't jibe with the openings called for in the electrical and plumbing drawings.

These are typical examples of lapses in coordination between architect and consultant, between consultants, and between the various building trades on the job. Most of the problems start with the drawings; here are the most effective ways to prevent them:

- Have all plan drawings by all disciplines done at the same scale and format, preferably through direct reuse of the architectural plans as background or base sheets. Then make transparency coordination check prints instead of relying on ordinary opaque check prints. There is no more effective way to relate and coordinate drawings of all disciplines than to see them in layers directly atop one another. Best of all, use a consistent overlay drafting system.

- Engineers' drawings, being generally schematic rather than literal, may mislead architectural staff as to the actual sizes of equipment to be installed. Don't let large amounts of ductwork, piping, and electrical work accumulate in one area without providing extra space for construction. Some equipment may fit dimensionally into the mechanical spaces, but manipulations required for installation may be physically impossible.

- Don't leave maintenance access to equipment to chance or guesswork. Provide generous, rather than minimal, hatchways, chases, and access panels. These will usually pay for themselves even before construction is completed by reducing difficult working conditions and simplifying inspection and adjustments.

Figure 6.1 The computer will assist in preventing environmental design errors. In this example a light fixture plan is graphically represented by a CADD system. (Courtesy of Steelcase, Inc.)

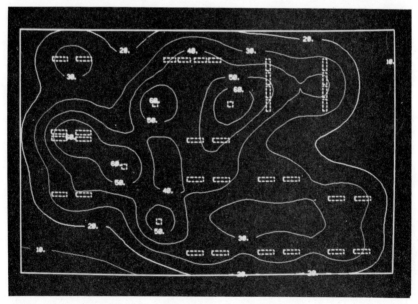

Figure 6.2 The lighting arrangement's net result relating to light distribution and intensities is charted out by the computer. (Courtesy of Steelcase, Inc.)

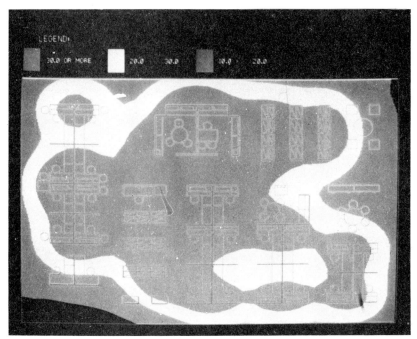

Figure 6.3 This photo is from computer screen color-coded CADD graphic output superimposed on the furniture arrangement. (Courtesy of Steelcase, Inc.)

Figure 6.4 The final result of the computer analysis. A presumably successful lighting plan. (Courtesy of Steelcase, Inc.)

Shortcuts for Preventing Visual Design Errors

"When showing a design, the number of blatant flaws will be proportional to the number of viewers."

—Murphy

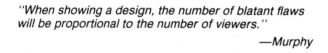

Familiarity breeds blind spots during any building design process. Some common results:

> • Much time is spent refining surface details that end up out of viewing range when the building is completed. Conversely, some elements given only passing attention by designers (such as roof penthouses and bulkheads on low-height buildings) turn out to be prominent visual features.
>
> • Some carefully proportioned buildings seem strangely distorted, diminished, or out of place when seen in the context of their overall surroundings. Distant background structures often have a strong impact that was clearly not considered by the designer.
>
> • Buildings change character and may look garish because of nighttime interior illumination—an effect that was not thought of because it didn't show up in design drawings or study models.

Designers have invented techniques for creating fresh new ways of looking at their work. These "fresh looks" catch visual trouble spots before others see the work, or worse, before the problems become built in. For example:

- Plans, elevations, and perspectives are viewed in a mirror or in reverse prints. If the design isn't symmetrical, the reversal gives a whole new impression and will show up discontinuities in design that design staff may have become blind to. The difference is sometimes startling enough that major points for improvement become instantly obvious.

- Elevations and perspectives are sometimes printed on negative paper to bring out previously unseen qualities. When rendered drawings have darkened fenestration in the original, for example, a negative print will show the approximate nighttime appearance.

- Details of trim, railings, fenestration, etc., sometimes change oddly in appearance and in scale relative to other parts of a building when they are enlarged to their full size. Some offices draw up full-size details, textures, material patterns, etc., on wall-sized sheets for study and refinement and to avoid surprises after construction. A few offices use opaque optical projectors as an economical means of achieving near full-size approximations from small sketches.

- Some top design firms put their building designs on the site photographically. The method is simple: Photographic color slides are taken of the site and later "back-projected" onto a matte acetate, polyester, or translucent polyethylene screen at the office. Study models (or pasteboard mock-ups of elevations) are placed in front of the rear projection screen and viewed at pedestrian-eye level. The setup of model and rear-projected site images is photographed in turn. This makes it easy to compare variations in positioning, proportioning, and color relative to actual site conditions. (You can also reproject the composite image onto translucent drawing media mounted on glass or plexiglas and hand-trace the image to make ultrafast, fully accurate perspective sketches or outline drawings for renderings.)

- Study and presentation models often mislead designers because of the habit of seeing them at bird's-eye level. Details are elusive, even when viewed at simulated ground level. Ten inches is about as close as you can get to a small model without distorted vision. Extra large models, for instance, ½-inch scale, are one answer and are used plentifully by a few design-conscious offices. But they're extremely expensive. A larger number of designers get inside and up close to their small models by using the "Modelscope." This is a miniature periscope that brings the observer's vision down to model ground level with "model-sized" perspective. Attachments for photography through the scopes are available. Modelscopes are carried by larger art and drafting supply houses, including the major mail-order suppliers.

Computers, Advanced Design Methods, and Data Base Facilities Management

"If you use a comprehensive, logically organized computer data base, you can reach the wrong conclusions with total confidence."

—Murphy

Over the next 3 to 5 years every tool, technique, and piece of working data in this book will be computerized. Some already are. For example the predesign and spatial allocation techniques described in Chapter 2 were originally designed for computer (particularly the famous CRAFT program). But since virtually nobody had access to computers in those days, systematic spatial allocation came to be used mainly as a pencil-and-paper design process.

Most of the basic predesign and planning steps of Chapter 2 are illustrated in computer output form in the sequence of illustrations at the close of this chapter. It is hoped that by the time this book is available, such spatial allocation software will be widely available, even for microcomputers.

The spatial rules—both rules of thumb and building code regulations—will also be on computer, as will the causes of design and construction errors. Also on computer will be the Predesign and Planning Checklist from Appendix B of this book along with other systems management checklists such as those currently published as Guidelines manuals.

All of the data of this book (and much more, of course) will be available as software either as parts of ready-made design programs or as individualized office design and data base systems. Some firms have been building their data bases for years. Most have barely started. This chapter will show you how to start and what to expect as you computerize your design practice.

The oldest types of architectural and engineering data bases are in-house boilerplate master specifications and standard construction detail files. Such systems don't qualify as real "data bases" in the technical sense because they don't include sophisticated multilayered filing, indexing, and retrieval systems. But they can be considered as analogous and as predecessors of what will become universally practiced architectural and engineering data base management.

Every architectural and engineering firm will structure its future office files—especially as the files are computerized—for three new data base functions:

1. To compile technical and design data needed to do improved building design and constructions—particularly such data as feedback from the process of doing projects. This is the *office design and technology data base.*

2. To document all the decisions and tasks performed on each particular project. This is the *project management data base.*

3. To record all that is knowable about each completed building as a guide for ongoing maintenance, renovation, additions, tenant and rental management, etc. This is the *facilities-management data base.*

The sections that follow in this chapter will describe the data base concept in more detail and elaborate on its ramifications in accelerated design, design management, quality control, and architectural and engineering marketing.

ORGANIZING ARCHITECTURAL AND ENGINEERING PRACTICE AROUND DATA BASE MANAGEMENT

Two exceptionally useful ideas began popping up in architectural and engineering offices in the early 1980s. The concepts are "data base management" and "documentation." As they sound, they are part of computerization, but they have uses and implications far beyond that. They are mainly tools for dealing with some of the most deadly flaws and problems that have plagued architectural and engineering practice for generations.

"Data base management" is the useful storage of information in so systematic a way that it's instantly accessible whenever needed. It's a little shocking to realize that the information that design professionals need in their day-to-day work is most often not immediately accessible and retrievable.

Most data we need are not at our fingertips. Much, if not most, of many a workday is spent poking through files, rereading old notes, hunting through journals and documents, making calls, attending meetings, talking to others, and on and on in order to track down information. All that activity usually pertains to one of the following steps:

1. Identify information that you need.
2. Locate it.
3. Retrieve it.
4. Verify its accuracy and completeness.
5. Revise, update, or correct it.
6. Combine and correlate it with other data.
7. Communicate or use the information to some purpose.
8. Refile it.

There are many subsets of these steps, and auxiliary steps, but this list covers the main sequence of most office tasks.

In effect, that's what most of us do for a living, day after day throughout our working lives. But to the degree we haven't known what it is we've been doing, we haven't done it very well.

It is all information processing, an activity that's central to all office activity. Most architects and engineers haven't perceived it as central to what they do. Thus information or data processing hasn't been given the attention it deserves as a professional specialty in its own right, as is financial management, for example, or working-drawing production. This oversight has led architects and engineers to miss some great opportunities and to suffer unnecessary problems. Here are some examples:

- The most common building failures are not due to failures in materials or to extreme conditions of some sort. Most failures in roofing, curtain walls, masonry, concrete, site drainage, fenestration, etc., are data failures. The physical causes of such failures are very well understood. The methods of preventing them have been widely publicized. But the information doesn't get to those who need it. Very few offices have a comprehensive, easy-to-use, technical data base. Even more telling, many firms are repeatedly taken to court for the same kinds of design, documentation, and construction failures. (It's customary to fire the people involved with projects that go sour. The underlying problems and data gaps thus remain uncorrected, so the same errors continue to recur.)

- Once, a semiretired architect-engineer told me that "systems" were pointless to him because "saving a few minutes" wouldn't make any difference in his work. An analysis of his practice over the previous 30 years showed that 30 to 40 percent of his work life—at least 10 years—was spent on rethinking, redesigning, and redoing drawings and notes that were already stored in his files. He didn't know what was on file or how to retrieve and reuse it. The raw material of a document data base was there but was never put to use. The net result: 10 years of laborious pencil pushing to recreate the same old information over and over.

- On a much larger scale, a nationally known architect has produced a series of buildings for various clients that feature massive construction elements—his "design trademarks"—that are repeated in almost every one of his buildings. Each major repetitive plan, section, elevation, and detail has been drawn over again each time. The fees wasted in repetitive drafting and supervision over 8 years amounted to at least $1 million.

- In all design firms, many of the same decisions are remade, virtually all the same steps followed, the same research done, the same trouble spots discovered, and the same problems solved over and over again on project after project. The duplication is not only repeated from past through future, it also takes place in projects occurring in the office at the same time. A typical example: Two senior drafters talking at a 1983 office Christmas party discovered each had spent months researching, designing, and detailing almost identical demountable partition systems.

What does data base management do? The opposite of all the above. Decisions, steps, research, problem spots, solutions, cost and time schedules (budgeted and actual), drawings, notes, and all other useful data are stored in such a way that all that hard-won information can be located and put to work on command, rather than reinvented on every new job. And the way this is done is to think ahead to all possible reuses and correlations of the data and to code it all accordingly.

Doesn't running a data base take extra work? And create more office bureaucracy? And produce mountains of useless records? It can. That's why data base management is a professional discipline in itself. However most of what's done with a systematically maintained data base is a normal part of office routine anyway, so there's not much added time investment. The old things are still done but in a more structured way.

This is where the parallel idea of "documentation" comes in. Documentation in this sense means thinking ahead to potential reuse of all information. Thus data are created, organized, coded, and stored in such a way that you not only can find and reuse that particular information but also have access to related data at the same time. For example, in calling up a construction detail, you should have options not only of getting the detail, but of retrieving a record of all jobs the detail has been used on, related and alternative details, the current cost of using this detail in construction compared with other options, the specification sections related to this detail, optional notation, sources of technical literature related to the detail, and so on.

Here are a couple of additional architectural and engineering practice illustrations: If you create production drawings, and at some point someone has to use those drawings to make a separate list of specification sections, then the work has been done twice. That list could and should be created automatically and simultaneously as the drawings are created in the first place. That's what data base management does. Similarly, if all the rooms of a building are named in the client's program, then lettered onto design development drawings, and later lettered onto working-drawing floor plans, and still later on finish schedules, then something has been done four times that should and could have been done only once using a data base.

Here are some more common questions:

- Isn't data base management just a glorified filing system? Yes, but the glorification is in the fact that every piece of filed data can be linked to large amounts of other data, as in the example of the standard detail which has a file number that identifies its history, notation, outline specification text, costs, alternative construction, related details, etc.

- Are computers an essential part of all this? Ultimately, yes. One of the major values of computers and electronic data processing is that they make it so convenient to store, index, cross-reference, retrieve, and reuse vast amounts of information that otherwise would involve mountains of paperwork. It's especially easy and convenient when the information is created on computer in the first place. If it isn't, there are still ways of organizing new project information as it is created that give it long-term value and expedite any later manual or computer storage and retrieval.

- How do you file all your design and technical data in such a way that it can be recaptured conveniently? The key is coding—a number system such as the Construction Specifications Institute (CSI) numbers for building components can identify every component you ever put into a building. And it can identify every material decision you ever make on any particular project—that is, every piece of equipment, every fixture, and every element of structure or finish is identifiable just by elaborating a bit on the specification numbering system that you are most likely already using.

A PRIMARY DATA BASE SOURCE— THE PREDESIGN AND PLANNING CHECKLIST

The Predesign and Planning Checklist (Appendix B of this book) is a special application of a data base. With the checklist, you run through options and choices that have to be made when designing a building. Each material design decision has a CSI-based identification number—rather like selecting building parts from a massive building parts catalog. (The short form list included in this book deals mainly with architectural features, however. The list of engineering components would take up more than this entire book in length.)

The Predesign and Planning Checklist is a start for the three main aspects of architectural and engineering data base management: your in-house office design and technology data base, the project management data base, and the facilities-management data base that can be created as a new postconstruction client service for each building project. As computerization takes hold, there will be numerous choices of software packages to assist with all this.

DATA BASE SOURCE NUMBER TWO— SERVICE SURVEYS AND POSTOCCUPANCY SURVEYS

A few architectural and engineering firms ask clients and client prospects to rate their work on "1-to-10"-type evaluation sheets. They report a high payback from such surveys.

Seems gutsy; who wants to risk hearing bad news? Emotional resistance to possible criticism is very high, and the use of evaluation questionnaires is correspondingly low. The fears are groundless, however. The great majority of people want to be genuinely helpful, not condemnatory. Potentially painful all-out negatives are rarely expressed.

Questionnaires are used to measure every major aspect of architectural and engineering service. Some firms ask client prospects to rate their brochures, responses to RFPs, presentations, and overall marketing effort. With minimal effort they gain thousands of dollars worth of advice, and they enhance their image with the prospects simultaneously.

After project completions, the firms ask for ratings of all major aspects of the service: dealings with regulatory agencies, design development, production, contract administration, and postconstruction services. Some firms list attributes of service and ask for client evaluations of such aspects as overall speed of service, responsiveness to special problems, quality of documents, professionalism of staff, and comparison with other firms the client has worked with.

Some firms have done postoccupancy surveys for over 20 years and now have a data base of design and construction dos and don'ts they consider to be among the most valuable assets of their practices. All they have done is collect the same information that's available job by job to any office, and by filing and using the information in a systematic way, they have turned it into a fortune in technical information, liability protection, and marketing value.

Of course many architects and engineers say their clients aren't at all shy about letting them know their complaints. Art collector Huntington Hartford, for example, let his architect, Ed Stone, know how he felt about their working relationship on a museum project by presenting Stone with a volume of reproductions of *The Horrors of War*, etchings drawn by Goya.

Still, when clients volunteer specific complaints or compliments at random, you're only getting a fragmented picture of your office's overall performance. More important, you're not getting a baseline of evaluation that you can use as a quantified standard both to motivate and to measure your future improvement.

There are two great rewards in client surveys: feedback and publicizing the fact that you care about what you're doing. One architect related that he saw surveys used in a New York office that instantly pinpointed long-festering staffing and communication problems. These were office-politics-type problems, where individuals managed to hide their deficiencies by passing blame to others. Clients had a much more accurate picture of who was doing his or her job well and who wasn't. Besides helping to open top management's eyes, clients responded to the opportunity of sharing their evaluations by bringing in new jobs.

Useful though the office performance surveys are, they don't build the long-term data base that can be the wellspring of a firm's design and technical expertise. The best long-term source is the postoccupancy survey—the systematic questioning of everything that works and doesn't work in an occupied building. "Postocs" are commonly conducted a year after initial occupancy, and, if an office is really thorough, they are repeated a year or two later. The questionnaires are varied for different users such as employees, management, maintenance personnel and include space for evaluating the performance of materials, lighting, HVAC, etc., much like the items originally listed in the user questionnaire described in Chapter 1.

By this time you can now detect a cycling and recycling of data gathering that occurs in data base management. One starting point of the cycle is marketing, which often opens with a diagnostic questionnaire review of a prospective client's needs. That information is fed into the office's data bank to assist in bringing forth existing prototype design information that the office has created over the years. Later that prototype design data will be updated and enlarged to the final design through client and user responses. And the updated technical data base will be used to refine the marketing diagnostic checklists.

Another cycle can be seen in construction detailing, where standard construction details that are likely to be needed are identified in design development by using the Predesign and Planning Checklist. As details are refined and elaborated upon for specific projects, they are upgraded by use of a job site feedback system which identifies problems with details that emerge during or after construction. That information is used to upgrade and enlarge the standard detail library and increase the choices that are possible during the Predesign and Planning Checklist stage.

As a client prospect is persuaded to move into a more advanced phase—predesign and programming—the questioning becomes more elaborate. It zeros in on specific users of the prospective building as outlined in Chapter 1. This leads to schematic spatial allocation diagrams and planning as described in Chapter 2.

The data accumulated from client performance surveys and postoccupancy surveys direct and refine both the design process and the future process of design data gathering. They can be thought of as systematic learning, learning from both mistakes and successes. In this interactive learning process, presumably the mistakes decline and the successes multiply.

Next we'll look at what promises to become the most important aspect of future architectural and engineering service—data base facilities management.

"LIFE AFTER DEATH"— FACILITIES MANAGEMENT AS A NEW SERVICE FOR DESIGN FIRMS

For years architects and engineers have largely overlooked an enormous potential source of design work. That source is facilities and property management.

Besides providing new design work, facilities managers can give you long-term renovation and maintenance contracts on their buildings. Those contracts make you the "house design firm" and lead directly back to major new building projects in the future.

Facilities managers can also give you a special kind of new contract: data base facilities management. A few computerized design firms already earn most of their income from data base facilities management contracting. Facilities management plus high-tech corporate construction is unquestionably the growth market for architects and engineers through the rest of the 1980s.

Data base facilities management (DBFM) is computer storage of all relevant information about buildings, including "as-builts." It includes furniture and equipment inventories, construction history, specifications, and ongoing maintenance records of everything from paint to plumbing valves. There's a vast amount of work to be had in this realm. For example, the Everett I. Brown CADD service bureau in Indianapolis reports that as of 1983 they were billing $5000 worth of drawings each month just to update the data base for one single corporate building.

If all this new work is out there, why aren't more architects and engineers going after it? Management consultants say it may be a combination of obsolete attitudes and slowness to computerize. Joe Ouye, a design consultant, suggests that "A/E's don't realize there's life after death." That is, the profession at large hasn't realized the implications of the fact that most of many buildings' lives—most of the design and construction—will go on long after the buildings are "finished."

Initial design and construction may take only 30 percent, 10 percent, or less of the total time, money, and effort that will later go into sustaining a building's long-term existence. But while design and construction continue on and on, the original project architects and engineers aren't involved. The project is "dead" to them, and usually they have long since put their drawings and specs into storage.

Why would architects and engineers want to do endless repairs, rehabs, and interiors work on old building projects? One reason: With a data base system the negative aspects of such work are greatly diminished. The work is comparatively easy because baseline data don't have to be surveyed and redrawn or recomputed from scratch each time. Like systems drafting and systems graphics, everything is there for fast, direct reuse and adaptation. Since the work is comparatively easy, yet of high value to the clients, it can be unusually profitable. Design firms that create facilities data bases for clients usually retain ownership of the data in their own computers. That gives them strength in later client negotiations. Architects and engineers have rarely enjoyed such strength in the past.

For more information on facilities management as a design specialty, get in touch with the leading organizations and publications. Some of these addresses may be obsolete by the time you read this book, but most any library can look up current data for you.

International Facility Management Association, IFMA, 3970 Varsity Drive, Ann Arbor, MI 84104

The Building Owners and Managers Association, Int'l., 1221 Massachusetts Avenue, N.W., Washington, DC 20005

The Institute of Real Estate Management, 430 N. Michigan Avenue, Chicago, IL 60611

Buildings Magazine, 427 6th Avenue, S.E., Cedar Rapids, IA 52406

Facilities Design & Management Magazine, Gralla Publications, 1515 Broadway, New York, NY 10036

AFTER TODAY'S COMPUTER REVOLUTION

What's the next big step after computers? Artificial intelligence (AI) for one. And, in the process, massive leaps in human understanding of our own intelligence.

IBM, Control Data Corp., and the United States and Japanese governments, to name a few, aren't satisfied with computers as they are. They, plus thousands of individual researchers around the world, intend to create machines that think—or at the least, machines that imitate thinking so well that nobody will be able to tell the difference.

An early product of this research has been new thinking about thinking and some radical theories. For example, Harris Walker, a physicist at Johns Hopkins says the human brain processes 1 trillion bits of data per second. (The "bit" is the irreducible elemental primary of all information. It's the electronic on or off switch that means "yes" or "no," "either-or.") Information of any type or complexity can be stored and processed as binary digits—bits—and 1 trillion bits per second adds up to a universe of information in a very small time package. This points to a potential human brainpower far more vast than ever suggested before, but recent estimates don't stop there.

A systems analyst at a Xerox think tank suggests that there's far more activity in the brain than anyone, including Dr. Walker, has suggested. He proposes that each neural cell probably processes 1 million bits of data per second in itself and that the data are "richer" because they are cycled in waves, with attributes of frequency, amplitude, and wavelength, thus carrying far more data than the linear off/on pulses that computers use. Since the brain is variously estimated to contain anywhere from 10 to 100 billion neurons, 1 million bits per second times 10 billion neural cells gives us data processing power of 10 quadrillion bits per second. This is a low-end estimate and will probably go up considerably.

To get a sense of what these numbers mean, translate bits to "bytes" (which means a single symbol or letter, usually made up of 8 bits), and "bytes" to English words of 8 bytes each on average, and the data flow I'm describing would be equivalent to 156 trillion words per second for the latter estimate. Walker suggests two-thirds of such activity is dedicated to subconscious activity such as endless recycling of all stored memory sensations.

The prospect of gaining self-awareness, self-control, and electronic imitation of this immense mental potential has computer and artificial intelligence theorists champing at the bit. Here are some current avenues of study:

- Some theorists believe that there are built-in patterns ("grids")— a sort of "machine language" of the brain—that translate all data (such as our ponderous spoken and written languages) into an internal code suited to the immense speeds of brain functioning. The search is on for subconscious languages or built-in grammar in brain structure that would allow us to think and communicate much faster.

- Many educators say we've been crippling children's brains in a barbaric school system. There's strong evidence that children can handle most primary schooling during ages 2 through 6 and complete their college work as preteens or in early adolescence. This isn't to be achieved by overwork and "surrendering childhood" but by allowing unrestricted access to data and free exercise of natural mental functioning. (Strongly expressed intellectual ambition among children is always referred to as a "problem" by teachers and administrators who currently dedicate a major part of school activity to keeping the problem contained.)

- Aesthetics and design theory may be seen in new light as a result of current brain research. The determinant of aesthetic success and failure may boil down to what most stimulates and augments intensified conscious activity. Success in visual design or musical composition may come from a consonance between a work's underlying patterning system and the internal receptor patterns already "hardwired" into the brain.[1]

[1]For background on these developments refer to (1) *Shuffle Brain*, by Dr. Paul Pietsch, Houghton Mifflin Co., Boston, 1981. This biologist, along with other leading brain researchers, now perceives the brain as operating as a hologram—a very readable book with revolutionary implications. (2) *The Enchanted Loom: Mind in the Universe*, by Robert Jastrow, Simon & Schuster, New York, 1981. Dr. Jastrow, founder of NASA's Goddard Institute, proposes that biological evolution is not the development of species into more adaptable forms but rather the evolution of one entity—the brain—in many types of animal bodies. He proposes the next stage of human evolution as a direct human linkage with computers.

Compared with past approaches, the main difference of concern in designing buildings as well as anything else for human use, may be a newly born awareness that we are designing for conscious entities of immense and largely unappreciated brainpower. Previous design criteria have centered on varied issues such as historic precedence, proportional and compositional values, social relevance, social status, natural environmental concerns, and even hygiene. If the criteria of planning and design become focused on that which enhances or enlarges human conceptual consciousness, we may expect to see a new level of care and respect for the human being who is, after all, the whole point of all design endeavor. We may also expect to see spectacular new environments that encompass all previous considerations and add to them on a grand aesthetic scale.

FUTURE MEDIA FOR DESIGN, DESIGN PRESENTATION, AND SIMULATED ENVIRONMENTS

The magic word is "digitization." Digitized sound, images, data storage, and communication are about to revolutionize design, documentation, and design presentation.

The revolution started with the first digital audio disk players. Their sound reproduction quality is unsurpassed in realism because the original music is encoded in molecular detail.

At about the time this book is published, we'll see digitized image recreation on large, flat video screens for televisions and computers. Then, digitized movie and still cameras that store images electronically instead of on silver emulsion photographic film. And then photocopiers that operate the same way and deliver multicolor, photographic-quality reproduction.

Replaced in all this will be standard disk and tape recording, photography, lithography, diazo printing, traditional CADD screen and computer storage systems. These will all be replaced by systems that outperform the old ones and yet are variants of just one single technology. That means that data which are digitally "photographed" will be directly reproducible by video as well as photocopier. *All* data we deal with—words, numbers, graphics, photos, photocopies, video displays, holograms, and sound—will be stored through the same medium.

One result of integrated media: Images, such as design studies, created on new videodisk CADD systems will give what is now unimaginably real 3-D-modeled picture quality; store text, sound, and technical data; and let you combine any part of the images with either real, existing surroundings or imaginary ones. That means designers will "sketch" with whole, realistic images in space instead of with lines on paper.

HIGH-SPEED TOOLS AND TECHNIQUES IN A NUTSHELL

In summary, the building design process properly starts with a list of attributes of the project. There's a hierarchy in decision making as shown in Chapter 1 that determines which decisions have to be made before others can be made. For example, if the building population isn't a given, it will be determined by building functions. Population and function determine circulation and equipment requirements. Building spaces are determined by a combination of function, population, circulation, and equipment. Building shape, height, and spans are determined by interior spaces as restricted by limitations of site and zoning. Shape, height, and span set the primary limitations of structure, construction system, and framing. And framing, construction, and structure set the limits of choices of final surface treatments and finishes. And, of course, every decision at every step of the hierarchical sequence is determined or largely influenced by finance.

All the steps and peripheral decisions just cited can, and will, be inputted on computer as an electronic interactive checklist.

When you begin project programming and predesign, you'll state a few basic conditions and the computer will then be able to draw some conclusions which it can feed back to you. Then it will go further with you, step by step, through the whole preliminary design process. For example, if you were starting on a school of a certain type and size, the computer would automatically assume you would use common structural spans based on standard classroom sizes. You'll confirm or modify the computer's assumption. Once class sizes and general budget are made known to the computer, it will assume a certain structural system and ask if that's what you want. You'll confirm or modify that. That's how it will go through the basic configuration programming phase.

Later when you input the result of client and user questionnaires that size special spaces and establish priorities of relationships between spaces, the computer will add in a few assumptions of its own, just as any designer would, and produce some schematic plans for you. As you, and the computer, reach agreement on HVAC, lighting, and the ceiling system, the computer will "suggest" an appropriate interior partition module and construction system. Door types, hardware, shelving, chalkboards, and numerous other items will be suggested by the computer as the design firms up.

If you decide you want a certain partition system that won't work well with the ceiling system, the computer will say so. Later, as decision making gets more detailed, if you decide on a fenestration system that created problems on a previous project, the computer will let you know about it.

Throughout the process, the computer will record dates, times, participants, and reasons for design decisions. It will provide printout alerting you of wide-ranging ripple effects of seemingly minor changes in the building plan. By the time the design is complete, the computer will have most of the data it needs to produce finished working drawings—or their electronic equivalent. In other words, it will provide documentation of the design, which is what working drawings were always supposed to be in the first place—just a record of design decisions.

The final "drawings" within the computer's storage will not just be passive documentation either. They will be a "smart" data base source that will feed the office's design and technology file, the project management record, and the facilities-management data base. (Before long, buildings will be smart too and will send operating data from internal sensors to the facilities-management data base.)

With regard to the facilities-management data base, every single item in the building will have long ago been numbered and recorded—along with its relationships to other items. Thus, later, if the building owner wants to know the consequences of moving a light fixture, that information will be immediately knowable. If a tenant wants to know tax or warranty data on a movable partition system, that data will be right on tap.

Marvelous as electronic data bases are, keep in mind that they don't create their data. You do. Even if you do not have access to computerized predesign, programming, CADD, etc., you can still generate the information that would go into such a system and use it as if you had such a system. You can file data in a systematic keycode fashion like that of the Predesign and Planning Checklist, and you can turn everything that you do in your design practice into permanent assets that can be improved and reused in different ways throughout the rest of your professional career.

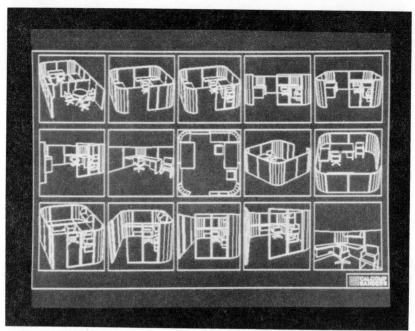

Figure 7.1 Furniture and office groupings can be created and then manipulated in the computer as single units. Here an office cubicle arrangement is viewed in perspective inside and out. (Courtesy of CalComp.)

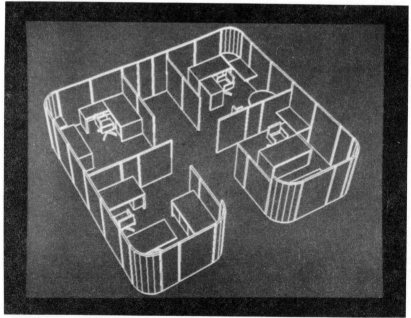

Figure 7.2 A composite of several office units in perspective. The image can be studied on the computer screen or drawn on the plotter for study or presentation. (Courtesy of CalComp.)

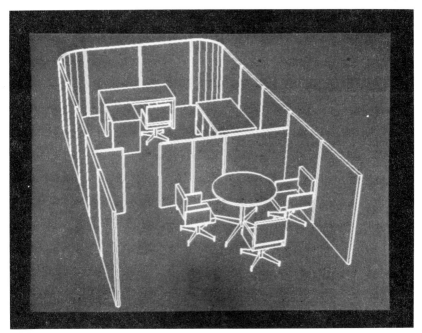

Figure 7.3 Every piece of furniture shown in these perspectives is identified by a catalog number. The facilities manager can call for printout that will tell how many of each item are in inventory, what rooms they are in, how much they cost, and what their present condition, estimated life, and depreciation status are. (Courtesy of CalComp.)

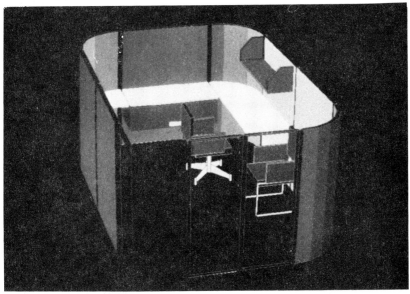

Figure 7.4 While the line drawings are adequate for considering the general disposition of furnishings and fixtures, a fully modeled, full-color 3-D image lets designers work with their final finish material and color schemes on the terminal. (Courtesy of CalComp.)

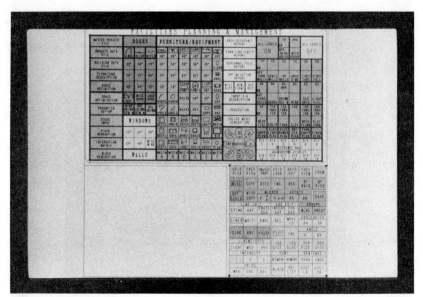

Figure 7.5 A typical menu, or macro, that lets the CADD operator call up any fixture, symbol, note, etc., previously stored for reuse. These expedite the original design and drafting of a facility and later act as a data base—a record of all the elements that have been installed in a particular building. (Courtesy of CalComp.)

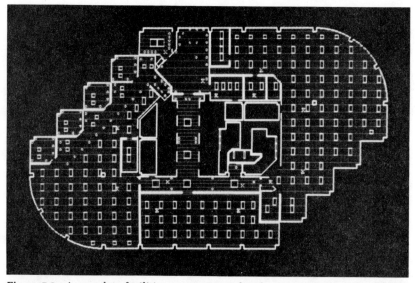

Figure 7.6 A complete facilities-management data base includes an identification number for every building element such as each light fixture in this reflected ceiling plan. Later, when the tenant or building owner wants to move a fixture or change an office space and has to rewire a fixture for switching, he or she can identify the fixture's number and get all relevant data as to circuitry, fixture source and cost, estimated life, maintenance schedule, etc. (Courtesy of CalComp.)

This Book Has a Hidden Agenda— "Design Management"

"Design consultants are mysterious people from out of town who ask you for numbers and then sell them back to you."

—Murphy

"Design management" is a whole new design profession, and it's making its public debut here, in this book.[1]

Design management deals with all that happens before a project is designed: project research, user interviews, programming and predesign, feasibility studies, site selection, and designer selection.

It deals with documenting and monitoring the design process: quality control, schedule control, budget control, recording the ongoing decision-making process, and it includes Value Engineering.

[1]The concept of design management as a distinct new profession was originated by Dr. Joe Ouye of Design Logic in Oakland. Dr. Ouye earned his doctorate in advanced planning methodologies, and besides being one of the finest instructors I ever had at the University of California, Berkeley, is one of the nation's leading experts on design and planning systems. His counsel has been a valued aid in producing this book.

117

It deals with what happens after a project is completed: postoccupancy surveys, monitoring of building material performance, maintaining of a facilities-management data base, and transfer of newly learned data back to a predesign and programming data base as a guide for future projects.

Isn't all this already done as part of normal design service by architects and engineers?

In a word: No.

For example, some building clients follow systematic programming and predesign processes. So do a few architects. But most don't. The extreme differences between systematic predesign and programming and traditional design were explained in Chapters 2 and 3.

Until now, building clients have not had professional representatives to keep tabs on their architects and consultants. In these days, when up to one-third of all insured design firms may be sued in a single year over lapses in quality control, the need for such external quality control services should be obvious. The wide range and prevalence of design lapses were described in Chapter 6 on environmental control failures.

The idea of storing the work and experience of a design firm in a central office data base, and adding new data as new lessons are learned, makes perfect sense to most anybody. But this is still virtually unheard of in most architectural and engineering firms.

The tools of the design manager include sophisticated interview and sampling techniques, computerized data base expertise, and advanced problem-solving methodologies ranging from informal brainstorming to highly structured Value Engineering. The creative problem-solving and troubleshooting tools are described throughout this book, and particularly in the chapters on problem-solving shortcuts.

Does this mean that this book was really about design management?

Yes.

Then why didn't we say so to begin with? Because before this book was published nobody knew what design management was. It's hard to sell a book about something nobody knows exists. Now the hidden agenda is explicit rather than implicit. I hope you now have ample reason to consider the need for and the immense potential of this new level of design service.

How to Use the Predesign and Planning Checklist

"Muddle increases as the square of the number of units involved."

—Murphy

Most client and architect or engineer misunderstandings, disagreements, forced arbitration, and lawsuits arise because there is no record of the who, and when, and why of the design process. Decisions are made, rescinded, revised, and remade—sometimes several times over on the same items. On top of that, the multiple waves of decisions and changes are sometimes made by different people who don't know when or why others went through the same decisions on the same items. Under those circumstances, it's no wonder there are usually misunderstandings and disputes as to who did what, when they did it, and for what reasons. That's why the Predesign and Planning Checklist was created.

This checklist consists mainly of sequential design decisions. It covers all stages of decision making, from the most general and tentative predesign decisions to detailed technical decisions that are often made during working-drawing production.

The checklist should be used during the first predesign and programming meetings with your client. Then it should be used again during schematics, during final design development, and, finally, as part of working-drawing planning. Much of your later use of the checklist will be for individual review and in meetings not only with the client but with other members of the design team, including your consultants.

Decision making has to proceed from the most general to the very specific because most specific technical decisions make sense only in the context of the big picture of the overall project. For example, it isn't going to make sense to decide on material finishes until you know the materials. And it usually won't work to select major construction materials without knowing the structural system. The structural system can't be firmly decided without knowing desirable heights, spans, and bay sizes. Heights and spans are determined by considering building occupancies and activities, which in turn are determined by the building's purpose and functions.

This checklist follows a layering, sequential approach to data gathering and decision making. Chapter 1, "Predesign and Programming—The First Steps," for example, started with the decision-making process for preliminary building sizing, configuration, structure, construction, and materials. Chapter 2, "Space Planning," showed how to get down to specific and objectively decided allocation of building spaces.

From there you can proceed through the introductory sections of the checklist with your client to establish the first wave of predesign decisions on everything from the quality of landscaping to the type and quality of air-conditioning.

As those introductory decisions firm up and move from the tentative to the definite, you can then proceed through more detailed portions of each checklist section. You and the client will become increasingly specific and technical in the decisions you make, until the overall building is logically established and well-defined.

Here are the step-by-step instructions for using the checklist pages:

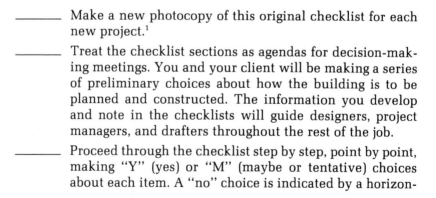

_____ Make a new photocopy of this original checklist for each new project.[1]

_____ Treat the checklist sections as agendas for decision-making meetings. You and your client will be making a series of preliminary choices about how the building is to be planned and constructed. The information you develop and note in the checklists will guide designers, project managers, and drafters throughout the rest of the job.

_____ Proceed through the checklist step by step, point by point, making "Y" (yes) or "M" (maybe or tentative) choices about each item. A "no" choice is indicated by a horizon-

_____
[1]Copies are for your personal use only, of course. Selling, trading, or giving copies of this text to any other person without permission is a violation of copyright and subject to legal penalties.

tal line. An "undecided" is marked by making a circle around the two lines under the Y and M columns.

_____ Make general decisions the first time or two through by marking generic elements at the top of each section. Each major subdivision of the checklist starts with a key design item such as exterior walls, roofing, or fenestration. Then each section within the major subdivisions opens with a general design or construction element such as fencing. The first and most general decision would be whether to use fencing or not in part of the project. That "Fencing" heading is followed by a list of types of fences. Your tentative or final choices of the specific type and treatment of the fencing may not come up until second- or third-stage reviews of the checklists.

Sample Checklist Section Heading:

	Y	M	WHO • WHEN • WHY	NOTES AND REVISIONS
FENCING	—	—	_____ • _____ • _____	_____
Cost category: __ A __ B __ C				

_____ As you make a general decision, such as choice cʃ a building element, you have the option of deciding the cost category or quality level of the item. If you and the client agree that the element is very important to the appearance of the project and that it deserves top-quality materials and workmanship, then it gets an "A" marking. If the product isn't to be top of the line but still should be of good quality, it gets a "B." And if the element is strictly utilitarian and of no great importance either for appearance or for security, it gets the "C" rating. These cost category ratings are a vital part of predesign decision making. You'll find your cost notes to be extremely helpful throughout the job, so include them if it is possible to do so.

_____ Identify the *who* in the decision checklists with initials or coded abbreviations. The purpose is to clearly determine later whether your client was primarily responsible for making a particular decision, or if it was mainly a designer's decision, or a tenant's, or a contractor's who might be participating in the design process, or a building official's, etc. If a decision is the consensus of everyone involved, that will be what is noted. Don't overlook the importance of listing who made the decision. One of the most common points of dispute and litigation is the question of who actually made which decisions.

———— Keep a log of the names of participants, dates, etc., whenever you hold group meetings that use the checklist as the agenda. A list of likely participants at design decision meetings, a suggested shorthand identification system, and a model Design Decision Review Log are all included at the end of this appendix.

———— Note by month and day the *when* of a decision, such as 6/9/83.

———— Note the *why* of the decision. Use the "decision code" we propose on page 126 of this section, or devise one of your own. As you'll see, the vast majority of decisions are made for only a few different reasons. Describe any special complex choices and their reasons in the "notes and revisions" column.

Sample:

	Y	M	WHO • WHEN • WHY	NOTES AND REVISIONS
FENCING	—	—	——— • ——— • ——	———————
Cost category: __A __B __C				
Chain Link Fence 02444	—	—	—— ———	——	———————

Who, when, and *why* are the most important parts of your job documentation. This is partly for reasons of legal self-defense and equally as a means of blocking unnecessary duplication of work and avoiding arbitrary design changes that may have unseen and unwanted consequences.

People often change prior decisions needlessly or incorrectly because they don't know the who and why of the original choices. For example, a yard fence and height might be changed in midproject by a drafter who is unaware that the original choices were a combined requirement of the building code and deed covenant. An associate design partner might notice a seemingly arbitrary choice of paving material and instruct a designer or drafter to change it. The associate doesn't know that the material is a mandatory requirement from the client and is not to be changed under any circumstance. These kinds of misunderstandings may occur hundreds of times on any project. This checklist will help prevent most of them.

_____ When decisions have to be changed, continue the check-listing process by lightly crossing out the choice that is being revised, and write the name of the change in the "notes and revisions" column. For example, if you change from a chain link fence to wood, the words "to wood" are all that need to be written in the revisions column. Add a note of the checklist page number that has the new decision if necessary. The who, when, and why of the revised decision will be noted on that page. Also, when writing a revised decision, add a note of what the previous choice had been, such as "Changed from chain link." If the change is revised again, say, from a wood fence to a brick wall, you'll follow the same procedure. This process leaves an "audit trail" through all the steps of decision making. Later, if people wonder why the yard wall is brick on the drawings instead of the chain link or wood fence they remember as being the choice, they can track down the sequence of change and the reasons for it. Best of all they won't assume the change is an error and mistakenly rescind it.

_____ Make more detailed and specific decisions on later go-rounds with the lists. Space is provided to note "materials/finishes/accessories" at the end of each list of choices. Note patterning, textures, coursing, special connectors or fixtures, and any other relevant aspects of treatment of the materials and products you have chosen.

_____ If decisions have been marked as tentative "M" for "maybe" or circled as "undecided," it means you need more data. To objectify the need for information, write a note in the "notes and revisions" slot. And to help assure that some action is taken on the matter, make a note of the date due and who is supposed to gather the data. Your "M's" and "undecideds" will be clear visual reminders of decisions that must be made before the job continues much further.

See the sample checklist format that follows.

Sample:

	Y	M	WHO · WHEN · WHY	NOTES AND REVISIONS
FENCING	—	—	——— : ——— · ——	———————
Cost category: __A __B __C				
Chain Link Fence 02444	—	—	—— —— ——	———————
Chain Link Gate 02444	—	—	—— —— ——	———————
Wire Fence 02445	—	—	—— —— ——	———————
Wire Fence Gate 02445	—	—	—— —— ——	———————
Wood Fence 02446	—	—	—— —— ——	———————
Wood Gate 02446	—	—	—— —— ——	———————

———— Note other work that may be affected by a decision.

———— Please note that as you make a decision on materials or construction, you automatically identify its CSI Masterformat–coordinated specification section number. That number can also identify standard details and standard notation or keynotes, as well as specification sections. This is your guide for later detailed planning and coordination of the working drawings and specs. (For the latest information on standard detail systems, working-drawing checklists, and standard notation and keynotes that are coordinated with this Predesign and Planning Checklist, contact Guidelines, Box 456, Orinda, California 94563, (415) 254-9393.)

Since the checklist is to be *the* job documentation record, you'll have to make sure people record any and all changes they make. If a person makes a change that should be recorded, but the checklist isn't available, she or he can write the change as a very brief "design change order" memo. For example, a project manager might receive a call from the clients saying they decided to accept a previously rejected concrete surface treatment after all. It isn't possible to locate and log that information in the checklist at the moment, so the project manager writes an equivalent memo with a note to transfer the change order data into the checklist as soon as possible.

SUGGESTED CODE IDENTIFICATIONS FOR "WHO" ON THE CHECKLIST FORMS

A suggested format for the list of names and codes for participants in the design decision-making process follows.

When a meeting is called, the particular pair or group of people present is noted at the top of the checklist. Then all decisions that are wholly joint decisions are noted "A" for "all."

When a decision is initiated as a specific preference or recommendation of a party, the originator of the decision is identified with initials.

Some users of checklists of this type have client decisions and agreements confirmed by adding an "approved" signature line for the client or client representative with each checklist section or page.

"Who" for Design Decisions and Choices of Products and Materials

PARTICIPANTS	INITIALS OR CODE
Owner	_____
Tenant	_____
Principal Architect	_____
Designer	_____
Mortgage Lender	_____
Loan Committee	_____
Regulatory Official	_____
Regulatory Board	_____
Engineers and Other Specialist Consultants	_____
_____	_____
_____	_____
_____	_____

SUGGESTED CODE IDENTIFICATIONS FOR "WHY" ON THE CHECKLIST FORMS

There are a limited number of reasons for any design decision. The dominant ones are aesthetics, building code requirement, cost, maintenance, user comfort, and simple personal preference of the architect, designer, tenant, or owner.

Here is a suggested code list of possible *whys*, with their corresponding abbreviations. Add any other reasons for design decisions you want, and modify the code in any way you see fit. Both a long- and short-form code are given.

"Why" for Design Decisions and Choices of Products and Materials

LONG-FORM CODE:

Aesthetic Value	AV	Local Standard Practice	LSP
Availability	AVA	Office Standard	OS
Code Requirement	C	Public Relations	PR
FHA	FHA	Safety	SAF
Fire	FIRE	Sanitation	SAN
Health	HLTH	Security	SEC
Building	BC	Site Relationship	SR
Zoning	ZC	Unstated Reason	US
Consultant Coordination	CC	(This last item especially requires a note of identification of *who*.)	
Convenience/Comfort for User	CON		
Cost (First Cost)	FC	SHORT-FORM CODE:	
Cost (Life Cycle)	LCC	By Client	BC
Durability	DUR	Consultant Coordination	CC
Easy Maintenance	EM	Design/Aesthetic Considerations	DC
Energy Conservation	ENG	Economics	EC

THE DESIGN DECISION REVIEW LOG

Each time a significant number of design items are considered either in individual review or in group meeting, make note of the job, date (and time if relevant), and participant or participants.

Note the sections of the checklist that are used.

Add any special event notes, such as notice of major changes in the client's design program, a change in design staff, notice of delay or temporary suspension of the project, or new deadlines.

The design decision form should be printed on your letterhead and follow a format similar to that shown on the accompanying sample log.

Design Decision Review Log

JOB IDENTIFICATION: _____

DATE: _____ TIME: _____ LOG ENTRY BY: _____

PROJECT PHASE: _____

REVIEW AGENDA: _____

CHECKLIST CHAPTER/SECTION: _____

PARTICIPANTS: PROJECT STATUS NOTES:

_____   _____

_____   _____

_____   _____

_____   _____

_____   _____

_____   _____

_____   _____

_____   _____

APPROVALS OF CHAPTER/SECTION DECISIONS:

Initials _____   Title _____

Initials _____   Title _____

Initials _____   Title _____

The Predesign and Planning Checklist

Contents

129

SITEWORK

	Y	M	WHO · WHEN · WHY	NOTES AND REVISIONS

DEMOLITION

Building Demolition 02060
Selective Demolition 02070
Demolition for Remodeling 02072

SITE PREPARATION

Clearing 02110
Structure-Moving 02120

SPRINKLER SYSTEMS
Cost: _ A _ B _ C

Underground Sprinkler System 02441
Aboveground Sprinkler System 02442

FOUNTAINS/WATER
Cost: _ A _ B _ C

Fountain	02443		
Fountain Pool	02443		
New Stream	02443		
New Waterfall	02443		

FENCING
Cost: _ A _ B _ C

Chain Link Fence	02444		
Chain Link Gate	02444		
Wire Fence	02445		
Wire Fence Gate	02445		
Wood Fence	02446		
Wood Gate	02446		

WOOD RETAINING WALLS/ PLANTERS
Cost: _ A _ B _ C

Wood Retaining Wall	02447		
Wood Planter	02447		

SITEWORK (cont.)

			Y	M	WHO.WHEN.WHY	NOTES AND REVISIONS

POSTS/BARRIERS
Cost: _ A _ B _ C

Lockable Post	02450	
Chain Barrier	02450	
Guardrail	02451	

BOLLARDS
Cost: _ A _ B _ C

Bollard	02451	
Concrete Bollard	02451	
Metal Bollard	02451	
Wood Bollard	02451	
Removable Bollard	02451	

SIGNS
Cost: _ A _ B _ C

Building Sign	02452	
Direction Signs	02452	

Traffic Signs   02452   _____
Poster Kiosk   02452   _____

TRAFFIC SIGNALS   02453   _____
Cost: _ A _ B _ C

BICYCLE RACKS   02457   _____
Cost: _ A _ B _ C

HANDICAP FACILITIES
Cost: _ A _ B _ C

Handicap Ramp   02458   _____

PLAY FIELDS   02460   _____
Cost: _ A _ B _ C

Play Yard   02460   _____
Sports Paving   02530   _____

PLAY EQUIPMENT
Cost: _ A _ B _ C

Playground Equip.   02461   _____
Play Structure   02463   _____

SITEWORK (cont.)

	Y	M	WHO.WHEN.WHY	NOTES AND REVISIONS

SITE FURNITURE
Cost: _ A _ B _ C

Bench	02471			
Seat	02471			
Table	02472			

PREFABRICATED SHELTERS
Cost: _ A _ B _ C

Prefab Information Booth	02473			
Prefab Guard Booth	02473			
Prefab Parking Attendant Shed	02473			

PREFABRICATED PLANTERS
Cost: _ A _ B _ C

Plant Tub	02474			

TRASH AND LITTER
RECEPTORS
Cost: _ A _ B _ C

Trash Receptacle   02475
Cigarette
Ash Receptacle   02475

SHELTERS AND BOOTHS
Cost: _ A _ B _ C

Bus Stop Shelter   02477
Shed   02478
Booth   02478

EXTERIOR DRINKING
FOUNTAINS
Cost: _ A _ B _ C

Drinking Fountain 02479

TREES, SHRUBS, AND
PLANTING
Cost: _ A _ B _ C

139

SITEWORK (cont.)

	Y	M	WHO·WHEN·WHY	NOTES AND REVISIONS

TREES, SHRUBS, AND
PLANTING (cont.)

Trees to Relocate 02481				
Shrubs to Relocate 02481				
Lawn/Grass 02485				
New Trees 02491				
New Shrubs 02492				
New Planting 02493				
New Ground Cover 02494				
Aggregate Planting Bed 02495				
Wood Chip Planting Bed 02496				

LANDSCAPE MAINTENANCE
SHELTERS
Cost: _ A _ B _ C

Landscape Maintenance Storage Shelter 02499				
Lath House 02499				
Greenhouse 13123				

STREET PAVING AND
SURFACING
Cost: _ A _ B _ C

Asphaltic
  Concrete Paving   02513 _____
Brick Paving   02514 _____
Portland Cement
  Concrete Paving   02515 _____
Asphalt Paving   02516 _____
Stone Paving   02517 _____
Highway Paving   02550 _____
Special Pavement
  Marking   02577 _____

DRIVEWAY PAVING AND
SURFACING
Cost: _ A _ B _ C

Crushed
  Stone Driveway   02511 _____
Asphaltic
  Conc. Driveway   02513 _____

141

SITEWORK (cont.)

	Y	M	WHO.WHEN.WHY	NOTES AND REVISIONS

DRIVEWAY PAVING AND
SURFACING (cont.)

		Y	M	WHO.WHEN.WHY	NOTES AND REVISIONS
Brick Driveway	02514				
Concrete Driveway	02515				
Asphalt Driveway	02516				
Asphalt Pavement	02516				
Speed Hump	02516				
Stone Driveway	02517				
Concrete					
Block Paving	02518				
Concrete Pavers	02518				
Gravel Surfacing	02519				
Special Pavement Marking	02577				

WALKWAY PAVING AND
SURFACING
Cost: _ A _ B _ C

Wood Plank Walk	02506				
Crushed Stone Walk	02511				

Asphaltic
  Concrete Walk   02513 ____ • • ____
Brick Walk   02514 ____ • • ____
Concrete Walk   02515 ____ • • ____
Asphalt Walk   02516 ____ • • ____
Stone Walk   02517 ____ • • ____
Concrete Pavers   02518 ____ • • ____
Tactile Warning
  Surface for
  the Blind   02539 ____ • • ____

PONDS AND RESERVOIRS
Cost category: _A _B _C ____

POND   02590 ____ • • ____
RESERVOIR   02590 ____ • • ____

MARINE WORK
Cost category: _A _B _C ____

SEAWALL   02883 ____ • • ____
JETTY   02885 ____ • • ____
BOAT DOCK   02890 ____ • • ____

SITEWORK (cont.)

DIVISION 3--CONCRETE

	Y	M	WHO·WHEN·WHY	NOTES AND REVISIONS

CONCRETE
Cost category: _A _B _C

Concrete Slab	03300
Concrete Retaining Wall	03302
Concrete Pergola	03450

DIVISION 4--MASONRY

UNIT MASONRY YARD WALLS
Cost category: _A _B _C

Brick Wall	04210
Adobe Wall	04212
Conc. Block Wall	04220
Concrete Block Retaining Wall	04228
Stone Wall	04410

144

DIVISION 5--METALS

METALS
Cost category: _ A _ B _ C

Handrails   05520 _____ | _____ : _____ | _____
Metal Trellis/ | _____ : _____ | _____
Lattice/Arbor/
Pergola   05725 _____ | _____ : _____ | _____

DIVISION 6--WOOD

WOOD
Cost category: _ A _ B _ C

Wood Decking   06125 _____ | _____ : _____ | _____
Wood Trellis/ | _____ : _____ | _____
Lattice/Arbor/
Pergola   06450 _____ | _____ : _____ | _____

145

SITEWORK (cont.)

DIVISION 9--FINISHES

	Y	M	WHO.WHEN.WHY	NOTES AND REVISIONS

FINISHES
Cost category: _ A _ B _ C

Tile Paving 09300				
Tile Finish Steps 09300				

DIVISION 10--SPECIALTIES

FLAGPOLES 10350
Cost category: _ A _ B _ C

IDENTIFYING DEVICES
Cost category: _ A _ B _ C

Freestanding
Directory 10411
"You Are Here"
Map Stand 10412

Bulletin Board   10415 _____
Sidewalk Plaque   10420 _____

PEDESTRIAN CONTROL DEVICES
Cost category: _ A _ B _ C

Turnstile   10450 _____

PROTECTIVE COVERS
Cost category: _ A _ B _ C

Covered Walkway   10531 _____
Car Shelter   10532 _____

POSTAL SPECIALTIES

Public Mailbox   10552 _____

TELEPHONE
ENCLOSURES   10750 _____
Cost category: _ A _ B _ C

SITEWORK (cont.)

DIVISION 11--EQUIPMENT

	Y	M	WHO·WHEN·WHY	NOTES AND REVISIONS
PARKING EQUIPMENT Cost category: _A _B _C			· ·	
Parking Gate 11151			·	
Paid-Parking Ticket Dispenser 11152			·	
Tire Spike Barrier 11156			·	
TELECOMMUNICATION EQUIPMENT 11800 Cost category: _A _B _C			·	

DIVISION 12--FURNISHINGS

	Y	M	WHO·WHEN·WHY	NOTES AND REVISIONS
ARTWORK 12100			·	

MULTIPLE SEATING
Cost category: _ A _ B _ C ___

Stadium/Arena
Seating   12730 ___

DIVISION 13--SPECIAL CONSTRUCTION

AIR-SUPPORTED
STRUCTURES   13010
Cost category: _ A _ B _ C ___

PREENGINEERED
STRUCTURES
Cost category: _ A _ B _ C ___

Buildings   13120 ___
Greenhouse   13123 ___
Grandstands/
Bleachers   13125 ___

SITEWORK (cont.)

DIVISION 13--SPECIAL CONSTRUCTION (cont.)

	Y	M	WHO.WHEN.WHY	NOTES AND REVISIONS

POOLS
Cost category: _A _B _C

Swimming Pool	13151
Wading Pool	13151
Jacuzzi	13153
Hot Tub	13154

LIQUID/GAS STORAGE
TANKS 13410
Cost category: _A _B _C

SOLAR ENERGY 13980
Cost category: _A _B _C

WIND ENERGY
SYSTEMS 13990
Cost category: _A _B _C

DIVISION 14--CONVEYING SYSTEMS

CONVEYING SYSTEMS
Cost category: _A _B _C

Sidewalk Elevator	14411	
Escalator	14710	
Moving Sidewalk	14720	

DIVISION 16--ELECTRICAL

EXTERIOR LIGHTING
Cost category: _A _B _C

Exterior
Building Light-ing	16520	
Light Standards	16530	
Walkway Lights	16530	
Lighting Bollards	16531	
Fire Alarm Box	16721	

151

STRUCTURE

    This checklist is different from the others in that it in-
cludes "Coordination Checks" which indicate other portions of
work that may be affected by decisions regarding the selection
of structural systems and members.

    Your preliminary structural design decisions will usually be
generalized, on the order of: "Concrete foundation, concrete block
bearing walls, steel joist roof." The options listed in this
checklist are similarly basic and do not deal with the many more
sophisticated structural options that are available to you.

PART ONE--FOUNDATIONS

	Y	M	WHO.WHEN.WHY	NOTES AND REVISIONS
PILES	02350		.	
Coord check:	civil/soils		cross sect	.
CAST-IN-PLACE CONCRETE	03300		.	

152

Concrete Footing   03305

Concrete
Foundation Wall 03306

Coord check: ____ civil/soils ____ util ____ plumb ____ drain ____ cross sect

        Y   M   WHO·WHEN·WHY   NOTES AND REVISIONS

UNIT MASONRY

Reinforced
Concrete Block
Foundation Wall   04230

Coord check: ____ civil/soils ____ util ____ plumb ____ drain ____ cross sect

        Y   M   WHO·WHEN·WHY   NOTES AND REVISIONS

PART TWO—LOAD-BEARING WALLS

LOAD-BEARING CONCRETE
WALLS

STRUCTURE (cont.)

PART TWO--LOAD-BEARING WALLS (cont.)

	Y	M	WHO.WHEN.WHY	NOTES AND REVISIONS
Concrete Wall 03316				
Precast Concrete (Structural) 03410				

Coord check: _____ elec _____ plumb _____ hvac _____ ext elev _____ cross sect

	Y	M	WHO.WHEN.WHY	NOTES AND REVISIONS
LOAD-BEARING MASONRY WALLS				
Brick Wall 04210				
Brick Pilaster 04210				
Brick Cavity Wall 04214				

Reinforced
Concrete Block   04230 _____

Reinforced
Concrete Block
Pilaster   04230 _____

Coord check: ___ elec ___ plumb ___ hvac ___ ext elev ___ cross sect

PART THREE--FRAMING

		Y	M	WHO·WHEN·WHY	NOTES AND REVISIONS
CAST-IN-PLACE CONCRETE FRAME	03300				
Concrete Slab	03300				
Drop Slab	03300				
Waffle Slab	03300				
Concrete Wall	03316				
Concrete Column	03317				

STRUCTURE (cont.)

PART THREE—FRAMING (cont.)

CAST-IN-PLACE
CONCRETE FRAME (Cont.)   Y   M   WHO·WHEN·WHY   NOTES AND REVISIONS

Concrete Pilaster 03317

Concrete Girder   03318

Concrete Spandrel 03319

Concrete Beam   03319

Concrete Joist   03319

Coord check: ___ elec ___ plumb ___ hvac ___ ext elev ___ cross sect

        Y   M   WHO·WHEN·WHY   NOTES AND REVISIONS

PRECAST CONCRETE   03400

Precast Panel   03411

Precast Deck   03412

Precast Column 03414 _____

Precast Girder 03415 _____

Precast Beam 03416 _____

Concrete Joist 03418 _____

Precast Prestressed
Concrete 03420 _____

Tilt-Up Concrete 03430 _____

Coord check: ___ elec ___ plumb ___ hvac ___ ext elev ___ cross sect

Y   M   WHO.WHEN.WHY   NOTES AND REVISIONS

MASONRY FRAMING

Brick Column 04210 _____

Concrete Block
Column 04230 _____

Coord check: ___ elec ___ plumb ___ hvac ___ ext elev ___ cross sect

STRUCTURE (cont.)

PART THREE--FRAMING (cont.)

Y	M	WHO.WHEN.WHY	NOTES AND REVISIONS

STRUCTURAL METAL FRAMING--VERTICAL MEMBERS

	Steel WF Column	05110				
	Tubular Steel Column	05122				
	Tubular Steel Post	05122				
	Concrete Filled Steel Post	05123				

Coord check: _____ elec _____ drain _____ hvac _____ ext elev _____ cross sect

Y	M	WHO.WHEN.WHY	NOTES AND REVISIONS

STRUCTURAL METAL FRAMING--HORIZONTAL SPAN MEMBERS

Steel WF Column 05110 |

Steel Girder 05115 |

Steel Beam 05116 |

Steel Truss 05119 |

Coord check: ___ elec ___ plumb ___ hvac ___ ext elev ___ cross sect |

Y   M   WHO.WHEN.WHY   NOTES AND REVISIONS

SPACE FRAMES 05161 |

Space Frame 05161 |

Geodesic 05162 |

Coord check: ___ elec ___ plumb ___ hvac ___ ext elev ___ cross sect |

Y   M   WHO.WHEN.WHY   NOTES AND REVISIONS

METAL JOISTS 05200 |

Steel Joists 05210 |

Aluminum Joists 05220 |

Coord check: ___ elec ___ plumb ___ hvac ___ cross sect

STRUCTURE (cont.)

PART THREE--FRAMING (cont.)

		Y	M	WHO·WHEN·WHY	NOTES AND REVISIONS
METAL DECKING	05300				
Metal Decking	05300				
Metal Roof Deck	05310				
Steel Roof Deck	05310				
Aluminum Roof Deck	05310				

Coord check: _____ elec _____ plumb _____ hvac _____ roof _____ cross sect

		Y	M	WHO·WHEN·WHY	NOTES AND REVISIONS
WOOD FRAMING-- VERTICAL MEMBERS					
Wood Column	06101				

Wood Post   06102

Studs   06110

Coord check: ___ elec ___ plumb ___ hvac . ___ ext elev ___ cross sect

Y   M   WHO.WHEN.WHY   NOTES AND REVISIONS

WOOD FRAMING--
HORIZONTAL SPAN MEMBERS

Built-Up
Wood Girder   06103

Wood Box Girder   06103

Wood Beam   06104

Wood Box Beam   06104

Wood Joists   06105

Wood Rafters   06106

Coord check: ___ elec ___ plumb ___ hvac . ___ ext elev ___ cross sect

STRUCTURE (cont.)

PART THREE--FRAMING (cont.)

	Y	M	WHO.WHEN.WHY	NOTES AND REVISIONS
HEAVY TIMBER				
Timber Truss 06131				
Mill Framing 06132				
Pole Frame 06133				
Coord check: ____ elec ____ plumb ____ hvac ____ ext elev ____ cross sect				

	Y	M	WHO.WHEN.WHY	NOTES AND REVISIONS
PREFAB STRUCTURAL WOOD				
Glu-Lam Girder 06181				
Glu-Lam Beam 06181				
Glu-Lam Decking 06182				

Wood Truss   06190

Coord check: ____ elec ____ plumb ____ hvac ____ ext elev ____ cross sect

INTERIOR PLANNING AND CONSTRUCTION

section begins on next page.

INTERIOR PLANNING AND CONSTRUCTION

DIVISION 3--CONCRETE

	Y	M	WHO.WHEN.WHY	NOTES AND REVISIONS
CONCRETE FLOOR Cost category: _ A _ B _ C				
(Other flooring, see: DIVISION 9--FINISHES)				
Concrete Slab 03300				
Concrete Topping 03320				
Concrete Slab 03356 Steel Trowel Finish				
Concrete Slab 03357 Float Finish				
Concrete Slab 03358 Broom Finish				
Concrete Slab 03359 Nonslip Finish				

CAST-IN-PLACE
CONCRETE WALLS
Cost category: _A_ _B_ _C_

		A	B	C
Exposed Aggregate Concrete	03351			
Tooled Concrete	03352			
Sand Blasted Concrete	03353			
Grooved Surface Concrete	03354			
Colored Concrete	03355			
Formwork Board Pattern Concrete	03356			

PRECAST CONCRETE WALLS
AND DECK
Cost category: _A_ _B_ _C_

		A	B	C
Precast Concrete	03400			
Precast Concrete Panel	03411			
Precast Concrete Deck	03412			
Tilt-Up Concrete	03430			
Decorative Precast Concrete Wall Panel	03451			

INTERIOR PLANNING AND CONSTRUCTION (cont.)

DIVISION 3--CONCRETE (cont.)

	Y	M	WHO·WHEN·WHY	NOTES AND REVISIONS

CEMENTITIOUS DECKS
Cost category: _ A _ B _ C

Gypsum Concrete 03310				
Precast Gypsum Plank 03515				
Wood Fiber Plank/Deck 03530				
Composite Concrete and Insulation 03540				
Asphalt and Perlite Concrete Deck 03550				

DIVISION 4--MASONRY

BRICK
Cost category: _ A _ B _ C

Item	Code	A	B	C
Brick Wall	04210			
Freestanding Brick Wall	04210			
Adobe Wall	04212			
Structural Glazed Tile	04213			
Brick Cavity Wall	04214			
Face Brick	04215			
Brick Veneer	04215			
SCR Brick	04216			

CONCRETE BLOCK

Cost category: _A_ _B_ _C_

Item	Code	A	B	C
Concrete Block Wall	04220			
Glazed Concrete Block	04221			
Exposed Aggregate Concrete Block	04222			
Split-Face Concrete Block	04223			
Fluted Concrete Block	04224			
Molded-Face Concrete Block	04225			
Freestanding Conc. Block Wall	04229			

INTERIOR PLANNING AND CONSTRUCTION (cont.)

DIVISION 4--MASONRY (cont.)

	Y	M	WHO·WHEN·WHY	NOTES AND REVISIONS

MISC. UNIT MASONRY
WALLS AND FINISHES
Cost category: _ A _ B _ C

Clay Facing Tile 04245				
Ceramic Tile Veneer 04250				
Terra-Cotta Veneer 04251				
Glass Masonry 04270				
Gypsum Masonry 04280				
Sound-Absorbing Unit Masonry 04285				

STONE WALLS
Cost category: _ A _ B _ C

Stone Wall 04400				
Rough Stone 04410				
Cut Stone 04420				

Marble 04422 —
Limestone 04423 —
Granite 04424 —
Sandstone 04425 —
Slate 04426 —
Cast Stone 04435 —
Flagstone 04440 —
Blue Stone 04441 —
Stone Veneer 04450 —
Marble Veneer 04451 —

DIVISION 5--METALS

METAL DECKING 05300 —
Cost category: _ A _ B _ C

METAL FABRICATIONS/
ORNAMENTAL METAL
Cost category: _ A _ B _ C

Metal Stair 05510 —
Ornamental
  Metal Stair 05710 —
Prefab Metal
  Spiral Stair 05715 —

DIVISION 6--WOOD AND PLASTIC

	Y	M	WHO.WHEN.WHY	NOTES AND REVISIONS

FINISH CARPENTRY
Cost category: _ A _ B _ C

Decorative				
Millwork	06220			
Laminated				
Plastic	06240			

ARCHITECTURAL WOODWORK
Cost category: _ A _ B _ C

Wood Cabinetwork	06410			
Wood Shelving	06412			
Wood Paneling	06420			
Wood Stairwork	06431			
Wood Workbenches	06453			

DIVISION 7--THERMAL AND MOISTURE PROTECTION

INSULATION
Cost category: _A _B _C

	A	B	C			
Rigid Insulation	07212					
Batt Insulation	07213					
Foamed-In-Place Insulation	07214					
Sprayed Insulation	07216					
Granular Insulation	07216					

DIVISION 8--DOORS AND WINDOWS

METAL DOORS AND FRAMES
Cost category: _A _B _C

	A	B	C			
Steel Door	08110					
Custom Steel Door	08112					
Aluminum Door	08120					
Stainless Steel	08130					
Bronze Door/Frame	08140					

171

DIVISION 8--DOORS AND WINDOWS (cont.)

	Y	M	WHO.WHEN.WHY	NOTES AND REVISIONS

WOOD AND PLASTIC DOORS
Cost category: _A _B _C

Wood Door	08210			
Flush Wood Door	08211			
Wood Panel Door	08212			
Plastic-Faced	08213			
Steel-Faced Door	08214			

SPECIAL DOORS
Cost category: _A _B _C

Access Door	08305			
Manual Sliding Fire Door	08310			
Powered Sliding Fire Door	08311			
Blast-Resistant Door	08315			

Item	Code
Security Door	08316
Kalamein (Metal-Clad)	08320
Metal-Clad Door	08320
Lead-Lined Door	08325
Coiling Door Overhead	08330
Coiling Door	08331
Side Coiling Door	08332
Coiling Grille Overhead	08340
Coiling Grille	08341
Side Coiling Grille	08342
Folding Door	08350
Panel Folding Door	08351
Accordion Door	08353
Flexible Door	08355
Overhead Door	08360
Vertical Lift Wood Door	08366
Vertical Lift Metal Door	08366
Sliding Glass Door	08370
Sound-Retardant Door	08380

INTERIOR PLANNING AND CONSTRUCTION (cont.)

DIVISION 8--DOORS AND WINDOWS (cont.)

ENTRANCES AND
STOREFRONTS   08400
(See Exterior Design and Construction)

	Y	M	WHO.WHEN.WHY	NOTES AND REVISIONS

INTERIOR GLAZING
Cost category: _ A _ B _ C

Fixed Glass 08800				
Plate/Float Glass 08811				
Tempered Glass 08813				
Wire Glass 08814				
Obscure Glass 08815				
Laminated				
Safety Glass 08822				
Mirror 08830				
Two-Way Sur-				
veillance Mirror 08835				
Plastic Glazing 08840				

DIVISION 9--FINISHES

METAL SUPPORTED
CEILING SYSTEM   09120
Cost category: _A _B _C

LATH AND PLASTER
Cost category: _A _B _C

Gypsum Lath and
Plaster Parti-
tion   09202

Gypsum Lath and
Plaster Ceiling   09202

Metal Lath and
Plaster Parti-
tion   09203

Metal Lath and
Plaster Ceiling   09203
Gypsum Plaster   09210
Veneer Plaster   09215
Portland Cement
Plaster   09220

INTERIOR PLANNING AND CONSTRUCTION (cont.)

DIVISION 9--FINISHES (cont.)

	Y	M	WHO.WHEN.WHY	NOTES AND REVISIONS

GYPSUM WALLBOARD
Cost category: _A _B _C

| Gypsum Wallboard Walls | 09250 |
| Gypsum Wallboard Ceiling | 09250 |

TILE
Cost category: _A _B _C

Ceramic Tile	09310
Ceramic Mosaic	09320
Quarry Tile	09330
Slate Tile	09332
Marble Tile	09340
Glass Mosaic	09350
Metal Tile	09380

TERRAZZO
Cost category: _ A _ B _ C

Portland
  Cement Terrazzo 09410 | | |
Terrazzo Bonded
  to Concrete 09411 | | |
Precast Terrazzo 09420 | | |
Terrazzo Tile 09421 | | |
Conductive
  Terrazzo 09430 | | |
Plastic
  Matrix Terrazzo 09440 | | |

ACOUSTICAL TREATMENT
Cost category: _ A _ B _ C

Acoustical
  Ceiling 09510 | | |
Acoustical
  Wall Panel 09511 | | |
Acoustical
  Ceiling Panel 09511 | | |
Acoustical
  Wall Tile 09512 | | |

INTERIOR PLANNING AND CONSTRUCTION (cont.)

DIVISION 9--FINISHES (cont.)

	Y	M	WHO.WHEN.WHY	NOTES AND REVISIONS

ACOUSTICAL TREATMENT (cont.)

Acoustical Ceiling Tile	09512			.	
Acoustical Metal Ceiling System	09513			.	
Acoustical Plaster	09520			.	
Acoustical Insulation	09530			.	
Sound Isolation Wall	09530 13080			.	
Acoustical Barriers	09530			.	

WOOD FLOORING
Cost category: _ A _ B _ C

Wood Floor 09550

Perimeter Expansion Strip 09550
Wood Strip Floor 09560
Gymnasium Hardwood Floor 09561
Gymnasium Steel Spline Floor 09562
Wood Parquet Floor 09570
Wood Block Floor 09595

STONE AND BRICK FLOORING
Cost category: _A _B _C

Flagstone Floor 09611
Slate Floor 09612
Marble Floor 09613
Granite Floor 09614
Brick Floor 09620

RESILIENT FLOORING
Cost category: _A _B _C

Resilient Tile 09660
Resilient Sheet 09665
Conductive 09675

INTERIOR PLANNING AND CONSTRUCTION (cont.)

DIVISION 9—FINISHES (cont.)

	Y	M	WHO.WHEN.WHY	NOTES AND REVISIONS
CARPETING				
Cost category: _A_ _B_ _C_				
Carpet 09682				
Bonded				
Cushion Carpet 09683				
Carpet Tile 09690				
SPECIAL FLOORING				
Cost category: _A_ _B_ _C_				
Resinous Flooring 09701				
Conductive Elas-				
tomeric Floor 09731				
Heavy-Duty				
Concrete Topping 09740				
Armored Floor 09741				
Laminated				
Plastic Flooring 09755				

WALL COVERING
Cost category: _ A _ B _ C

Vinyl-Coated
  Fabric   09951
Vinyl   09952
Cork   09953
Fabric   09955
Wood Sheet/Veneer 09960
Prefinished
  Panels   09970

DIVISION 10--SPECIALTIES

                                        Y   M   WHO.WHEN.WHY   NOTES AND REVISIONS

CHALKBOARDS/TACKBOARDS
Cost category: _ A _ B _ C

Chalkboard   10110
Tackboard   10120

SERVICE WALL
SYSTEMS   10250
Cost category: _ A _ B _ C

INTERIOR PLANNING AND CONSTRUCTION   (cont.)

DIVISION 10--SPECIALTIES   (cont.)

	Y	M	WHO·WHEN·WHY	NOTES AND REVISIONS

ACCESS FLOORING   10270
Cost category: _A _B _C

FIREPLACES AND STOVES
Cost category: _A _B _C

Prefab Fireplace   10301
Stove   10320

IDENTIFYING DEVICES
Cost category: _A _B _C

Directory   10411
Bulletin Board   10415
Plaque   10420
Architect's
Plaque   10420

Illuminated Sign 10430
Sign 10440
Fire Exit Sign 10455

LOCKERS
Cost category: _A _B _C

Workbench Locker 10500
Wardrobe Locker 10501
Box Lockers 10502
Basket Lockers 10503
Coin Lockers 10505
Locker Bench 10510

FIRE EXTINGUISHER
CABINETS/ACCESSORIES
Cost category: _A _B _C

Fire Extinguisher
Cabinet 10522
Fire Blankets 10523

INTERIOR PLANNING AND CONSTRUCTION (cont.)

DIVISION 10--SPECIALTIES (cont.)

	Y	M	WHO.WHEN.WHY	NOTES AND REVISIONS
POSTAL SPECIALTIES Cost category: _ A _ B _ C				
Mail Chute 10551				
Mailbox 10552				
PARTITIONS Cost category: _ A _ B _ C				
Mesh Partition 10601				
Demountable Partition 10610				
Stud-Type Movable Partition 10613				
Movable Gypsum Partition 10616				
Movable Metal Partition 10617				

FOLDING PARTITIONS
Cost category: _ A _ B _ C

| | | | | |
Folding Partition 10620 | | | |
Accordian Folding | | | |
  Partition 10623 | | | |
Folding Gate 10624 | | | |

STORAGE SHELVING
Cost category: _ A _ B _ C

Metal | | | |
  Storage Shelf 10671 | | | |
  Wire Shelf 10673 | | | |

TELEPHONE ENCLOSURES
Cost category: _ A _ B _ C

Telephone Booth 10751 | | | |
Telephone Shelf 10753 | | | |

WARDROBE 10900
Cost category: _ A _ B _ C

INTERIOR PLANNING AND CONSTRUCTION   (cont.)

DIVISION 11--EQUIPMENT

	Y	M	WHO·WHEN·WHY	NOTES AND REVISIONS
MAINTENANCE EQUIPMENT 11010 (See Appurtenances Section)				
SECURITY AND VAULT EQUIPMENT Cost category: _A _B _C				
Vault Door/Day Gates 11021				
Service/Teller Window Unit 11022				
Package Transfer Unit 11023				
Security/Emergency System 11024				
Automatic Teller 11025				
Depository Slot 11026				
Depository Box 11026				
Wall Safe 11028				
Floor Safe 11028				

CHECKROOM
EQUIPMENT   11030
Cost category: _A _B _C

LIBRARY EQUIPMENT 11050
Cost category: _A _B _C

THEATER/STAGE
EQUIPMENT   11060
Cost category: _A _B _C

MUSICAL EQUIPMENT 11070
Cost category: _A _B _C

MERCANTILE
EQUIPMENT
Cost category: _A _B _C

Display Cases   11101

VENDING EQUIPMENT 11120
Cost category: _A _B _C

187

INTERIOR PLANNING AND CONSTRUCTION (cont.)

DIVISION 11--EQUIPMENT (cont.)

	Y	M	WHO.WHEN.WHY	NOTES AND REVISIONS

AUDIOVISUAL
EQUIPMENT
Cost category: _A _B _C

Projection Screen 11131				
Projector 11132				
Projector Booth 11133				

PARKING EQUIPMENT
Cost category: _A _B _C

Parking Gate 11151				
Ticket Dispenser 11152				
Key/Card				
Control Unit 11153				
Coin Machine Unit 11154				

LOADING DOCK
EQUIPMENT   11160
(See Exterior Design
and Construction)

WASTE-HANDLING
EQUIPMENT
Cost category: _ A _ B _ C

Waste Compactor   11172
Pulping System   11174
Waste Collector/
Chute   11175

FOOD SERVICE
EQUIPMENT
Cost category: _ A _ B _ C

Cooking Equipment 11410
Washing Equipment 11411

RESIDENTIAL
EQUIPMENT
Cost category: _ A _ B _ C

INTERIOR PLANNING AND CONSTRUCTION   (cont.)

DIVISION 11--EQUIPMENT   (cont.)

	Y	M	WHO.WHEN.WHY	NOTES AND REVISIONS

RESIDENTIAL
EQUIPMENT (cont.)

Kitchen	11451			
Laundry	11452			
Disappearing Stairs	11454			

UNIT KITCHEN
CABINETS   11460
Cost category: _ A _ B _ C

DARKROOM EQUIPMENT
Cost category: _ A _ B _ C

Revolving Door	11471			
Transfer Cabinet	11472			
Processing Equipment	11474			

ATHLETIC/
RECREATIONAL/
THERAPEUTIC EQUIPMENT
Cost category: _ A _ B _ C

Gymnasium
 Equipment   11486
 Therapy Equipment 11490

INDUSTRIAL AND
PROCESS EQUIPMENT 11500
Cost category: _ A _ B _ C

LABORATORY
EQUIPMENT   11600
Cost category: _ A _ B _ C

MEDICAL EQUIPMENT 11700
Cost category: _ A _ B _ C

TELECOMMUNICATION
EQUIPMENT   11800
Cost category: _ A _ B _ C

191

INTERIOR DESIGN AND CONSTRUCTION (cont.)

DIVISION 12--FURNISHINGS

	Y	M	WHO.WHEN.WHY	NOTES AND REVISIONS

ARTWORK

Mural	12110				
Sculpture	12140				
Statuary	12140				
Bas-Relief	12150				
Stained Glass	12170				

MANUFACTURED CABINETS
AND CASEWORK
Cost category: _A _B _C

Metal Casework/					
Cabinets	12301				
Wood Casework/					
Cabinets	12302				
Built-In Table	12303				
Display Casework	12380				

WINDOW TREATMENT

Cost category: _A_ _B_ _C

		A	B	C
Valance	12503			
Blind	12510			
Vertical-Louver Blind	12511			
Horizontal-Louver Blind	12512			
Shades	12513			
Interior Shutters	12527			

FURNITURE AND ACCESSORIES

Cost category: _A_ _B_ _C

		A	B	C
Landscape Partition	12610			
Room Divider	12615			

RUGS AND MATS

Cost category: _A_ _B_ _C

		A	B	C
Foot Grille	12672			
Recessed Frame for Floor Mat	12673			
Floor Mat	12675			

INTERIOR DESIGN AND CONSTRUCTION (cont.)

DIVISION 12--FURNISHINGS (cont.)

	Y	M	WHO.WHEN.WHY	NOTES AND REVISIONS

MULTIPLE SEATING
Cost category: _ A _ B _ C _____ | ___ | ___ | _._ | _____

Auditorium/Theater
Seating   12710 ___ | ___ | _._ |
Multiuse Fixed
Seating   12750 ___ | ___ | _._ |

INTERIOR PLANTERS 12815 ___
Cost category: _ A _ B _ C ___ | ___ | _._ | _____

DIVISION 13--SPECIAL CONSTRUCTION

CLEAN ROOMS   13040 ___
Cost category: _ A _ B _ C ___ | ___ | _._ | _____

INSULATED ROOMS
Cost category: _ A _ B _ C ___ | ___ | _._ | _____

Cold Storage 13061

INTEGRATED
CEILING 13070
Cost category: _A _B _C

SOUND, VIBRATION,
AND SEISMIC CONTROL
Cost category: _A _B _C

Isolation Slab 13080

RADIATION
SHIELDING 13090
Cost category: _A _B _C

SPECIAL-PURPOSE
ROOMS/BUILDINGS
Cost category: _A _B _C

Prefab Steam Bath 13131
Prefab Sauna 13131

INTERIOR DESIGN AND CONSTRUCTION   (cont.)

DIVISION 13--SPECIAL CONSTRUCTION   (cont.)

	Y	M	WHO.WHEN.WHY	NOTES AND REVISIONS

VAULTS   13140
Cost category: _ A _ B _ C

POOLS
Cost category: _ A _ B _ C

Swimming Pool 13151
Aquaria   13152
Jacuzzi   13153
Hot Tub   13154

DIVISION 14--CONVEYING SYSTEMS

DUMBWAITERS   14100
Cost category: _ A _ B _ C

ELEVATORS
Cost category: _ A _ B _ C

Elevator   14210 _____
Freight Elevator 14220 _____

HOISTS/CRANES
Cost category: _A _B _C

Hoist   14300 _____
Crane   14300 _____

LIFTS
Cost category: _A _B _C

People Lift   14410 _____
Sidewalk Lift   14411 _____
Wheelchair Lift 14415 _____
Vehicle Lift   14450 _____

MATERIAL-HANDLING
SYSTEMS
Cost category: _A _B _C

Chute   14560 _____
Laundry Chute   14560 _____
Pneumatic Tube 14581 _____

197

INTERIOR PLANNING AND CONSTRUCTION   (cont.)

DIVISION 14--CONVEYING SYSTEMS (cont.)

	Y	M	WHO.WHEN.WHY	NOTES AND REVISIONS
TURNTABLE 14600				
Cost category: _ A _ B _ C				
MOVING STAIRS/WALKS				
Cost category: _ A _ B _ C				
Escalator 14710				
Moving Walk 14720				
DIVISION 15--MECHANICAL				
PLUMBING FIXTURES				
Cost category: _ A _ B _ C				
Watercooler 15455				
Wash Fountain 15456				
Shower 15457				
Tub Enclosure 15459				

Shower Enclosure	15459	
Drinking Fountain	15461	
Lavatory	15471	
Floor Sink	15475	
Janitor's Sink	15476	
Work Sink	15481	

LIQUID HEAT TRANSFER
Cost category: _ A _ B _ C

Radiant Panel	15745	
Baseboard Unit	15751	
Finned Tube	15752	
Convector	15733	
Radiator	15754	
Unit Heater	15760	
	16850	
Fan Coil Unit	15761	
Unit Ventilator	15762	
	16850	
Humidifier	15781	

INTERIOR PLANNING AND CONSTRUCTION   (cont.)

DIVISION 16--ELECTRICAL

	Y	M	WHO.WHEN.WHY	NOTES AND REVISIONS

COMMUNICATIONS
Cost category: _A _B _C

Burglar Detector	16720			
Fire Detector	16721			
Fire Alarm	16721			
Smoke Detector	16725			
Burglar Alarm	16727			
Clock	16730			
Telephone				
Switching Closet	16740			
Telephone				
Panelboard	16740			
Telephone				
Wiring Chase	16740			
Speaker	16770			
Annunciator	16770			
Closed Circuit TV	16780			
Surveillance TV	16780			

HEATING AND COOLING

Cost category: _A _B _C

	A	B	C
Electric Heating Coils	16860		
Electric Baseboard	16865		
Packaged Room Air Conditioner	16870		
Radiant Heater	16880		
Electric Heater	16890		

LIGHTING

Cost category: _A _B _C

	A	B	C
Fluorescent Fixture	16501		
Light Diffuser	16501 / 09120		
Spotlight	16501		
Chandelier	16501		
Surface-Mounted Light Fixture	16510		
Recessed Light	16510		
Luminous Ceiling	16515 / 09120		

INTERIOR PLANNING AND CONSTRUCTION (cont.)

DIVISION 16--ELECTRICAL

	Y	M	WHO.WHEN.WHY	NOTES AND REVISIONS

ELECTRICAL FIXTURES AND SYSTEMS
Cost category: _ A _ B _ C

Electromagnetic Shielding	16650	
Ceiling-Hung Clock	16730	
Ceiling-Mounted TV Camera	16780	
Ceiling-Mounted TV Monitor	16780	

EXTERIOR DESIGN AND CONSTRUCTION

section begins on next page.

203

EXTERIOR DESIGN AND CONSTRUCTION

DIVISION 3--CONCRETE

	Y	M	WHO.WHEN.WHY	NOTES AND REVISIONS

CAST-IN-PLACE
CONCRETE WALLS
Cost category: _A _B _C

Exposed Aggregate
 Concrete   03351
Tooled Concrete   03352
Sandblasted
 Concrete   03353
Grooved-Surface
 Concrete   03354
Colored Concrete   03355
Formwork Board
 Pattern Concrete 03356

PRECAST CONCRETE WALLS
Cost category: _A _B _C

Precast Concrete 03400
Precast
  Concrete Panel 03411
Tilt-Up Concrete 03430
Decorative
Precast Concrete
  Wall Panel 03451

DIVISION 4—MASONRY

BRICK
Cost category: _A _B _C

Brick Wall 04210
Freestanding
  Brick Wall 04210
Adobe Wall 04212
Structural
  Glazed Tile 04213
Brick
  Cavity Wall 04214
Face Brick 04215
Brick Veneer 04215
SCR Brick 04216

205

EXTERIOR DESIGN AND CONSTRUCTION (cont.)

DIVISION 4--MASONRY (cont.)

		Y	M	WHO.WHEN.WHY	NOTES AND REVISIONS

CONCRETE BLOCK
Cost category: _ A _ B _ C

Concrete Block Wall	04220				
Glazed Concrete Block	04221				
Exposed Aggregate Concrete Block	04222				
Split-Face Concrete Block	04223				
Fluted Concrete Block	04224				
Molded-Face Concrete Block	04225				
Freestanding Concrete Block Wall	04229				

MISC. UNIT MASONRY
WALLS AND FINISHES
Cost category: _ A _ B _ C

Wall Substructure: _____

Clay Facing Tile 04245 _____
Ceramic
  Tile Veneer   04250 _____
Terra-Cotta
  Veneer   04251 _____
Glass Unit
  Masonry   04270 _____

STONE WALL
Cost category: _ A _ B _ C

Wall Substructure: _____

Rough Stone 04410 _____
Cut Stone   04420 _____
Marble   04422 _____

EXTERIOR DESIGN AND CONSTRUCTION (cont.)

DIVISION 4--MASONRY (cont.)

	Y	M	WHO.WHEN.WHY	NOTES AND REVISIONS

STONE WALL (cont.)

Limestone	04423				
Granite	04424				
Sandstone	04425				
Slate	04426				
Cast Stone	04435				
Flagstone	04440				
Blue Stone	04441				
Stone Veneer	04450				
Marble Veneer	04451				

DIVISION 5--METALS

METALS
Cost category: _ A _ B _ C

Stainless Steel	05011				
Bronze	05012				
Aluminum	05013				

METAL FABRICATIONS
Cost category: _ A _ B _ C

Metal Stair	05510			
Metal Railing	05520			

ORNAMENTAL METAL
Cost category: _ A _ B _ C

Weather Vane	05700			
Ornamental Stair	05710			
Ornamental Hand-rails/Railings	05720			
Metal Trellis/Lattice/Arbor/Pergola	05725			
Metal Soffit	05730			
Metal Fascia	05730			

DIVISION 6--WOOD AND PLASTIC

FINISH CARPENTRY
Cost category: _ A _ B _ C

Wood Trim	06220			
Wood Shutters	06235			

EXTERIOR DESIGN AND CONSTRUCTION (cont.)

DIVISION 6--WOOD AND PLASTIC (cont.)

Y   M   WHO.WHEN.WHY   NOTES AND REVISIONS

ARCHITECTURAL WOODWORK
Cost category: _ A _ B _ C

Wood Soffit   06420
Wood Paneling   06420
Wood Fascia   06420
Wood Stair   06431
Wood Railing   06440
Wood Trellis/
Lattice/Arbor/
Pergola   06450

DIVISION 7--THERMAL AND MOISTURE PROTECTION

SHINGLES AND
TILES AS SIDING
Cost category: _ A _ B _ C

Item	Code	A	B	C
Asphalt Shingles	07311			
Wood Shingles/ Shakes	07313			
Slate Shingles	07314			
Metal Shingles	07316			
Clay Tiles	07321			
Concrete Tiles	07322			

PREFORMED SIDING
Cost category: _A_ _B_ _C_

Item	Code	A	B	C
Preformed Metal Panels	07410			
Preformed Metal Siding	07411			
Composite Panels	07420			
Cladding	07460			
Wood Siding	07461			
Composition Siding	07462			
Asbestos-Cement Siding	07463			
Plastic Siding	07464			
Plywood Siding	07465			
Aluminum Siding	07466			

211

EXTERIOR DESIGN AND CONSTRUCTION (cont.)

DIVISION 8--DOORS AND WINDOWS

		Y	M	WHO.WHEN.WHY	NOTES AND REVISIONS

ENTRANCES
AND STOREFRONTS
Cost category: _ A _ B _ C

Integrated Storefront	08400
Aluminum Entrance/ Storefront	08410
Automatic Entrance Door	08425
Revolving Door	08450

STEEL WINDOW   08510
Cost category: _ A _ B _ C

Steel Awning/ Projected Window	08511
Steel Casement	08512
Steel Pivoted Window	08515

ALUMINUM WINDOW 08520
Cost category: _A _B _C

Aluminum Awning/
Projected Window 08521
Aluminum
Casement Window 08522
Aluminum Double-
Hung Window 08523
Aluminum
Pivoted Window 08525
Aluminum
Sliding Window 08527

WOOD WINDOW 08610
Cost category: _A _B _C

Wood Awning/
Projected Window 08611
Wood
Casement Window 08612
Wood Double-Hung
Window 08613
Wood
Pivoted Window 08615
Wood
Sliding Window 08617

213

EXTERIOR DESIGN AND CONSTRUCTION   (cont.)

DIVISION 8--DOORS AND WINDOWS   (cont.)

	Y	M	WHO.WHEN.WHY	NOTES AND REVISIONS
GLAZING				
Cost category: _A_ _B_ _C_				
Fixed Glass 08800				
Double Glazing 08802				
Plate/Float Glass 08813				
Tempered Glass 08813				
Wire Glass 08814				
Obscure Glass 08815				
Spandrel Glass 08817				
Laminated				
Safety Glass 08822				
Insulating Glass 08823				
Mirror Glass 08830				
Plastic Glazing 08840				
GLAZED				
CURTAIN WALL 08900				
Cost category: _A_ _B_ _C_				
Glazed Steel				
Curtain Wall 08911				

Glazed Aluminum
  Curtain Wall   08912   _____·_____
Glazed Stainless Steel
  Curtain Wall   08913   _____·_____
Glazed Bronze
  Curtain Wall   08914   _____·_____
Glazed Wood
  Curtain Wall   08915   _____·_____
Translucent Wall
  System   08920   _____·_____

DIVISION 9--FINISHES

LATH AND PLASTER
Cost category: _A _B _C   _____·_____
Adobe Finish   09225   _____·_____
Stucco   09230   _____·_____

TILE
Cost category: _A _B _C   _____·_____
Tile   09300   _____·_____
Ceramic Tile   09310   _____·_____

215

EXTERIOR DESIGN AND CONSTRUCTION (cont.)

DIVISION 9--FINISHES (cont.)

	Y	M	WHO.WHEN.WHY	NOTES AND REVISIONS
TILE (cont.)				
Ceramic Mosaic 09320				
Quarry Tile 09330				
Slate Tile 09332				
Marble Tile 09340				
Glass Mosaic 09350				
TERRAZZO				
Cost category: _ A _ B _ C				
Terrazzo Tile 09421				
SPECIAL COATINGS				
Cost category: _ A _ B _ C				
Cementitious Coating 09820				
Textured Plastic Coating 09835				

Fire-Resistant
    Paint   09840 _____
    Antigraffiti
    Coating   09860 _____

DIVISION 10--SPECIALTIES

GRILLES AND SCREENS
Cost category: _A _B _C _____

Grille/screen   10240 _____
Security
Window Guard   10240 _____

PREFABRICATED STEEPLES,
SPIRES/CUPOLAS
Cost category: _A _B _C _____

Steeple   10341 _____
Spire   10342 _____
Cupola   10343 _____

EXTERIOR DESIGN AND CONSTRUCTION (cont.)

DIVISION 10--SPECIALTIES (cont.)

	Y	M	WHO.WHEN.WHY	NOTES AND REVISIONS

FLAGPOLES
Cost category: _ A _ B _ C

Wall-Mounted Flagpole	10350			
Roof Flagpole	10350			

IDENTIFYING DEVICES
Cost category: _ A _ B _ C

Directory	10411			
Bulletin Board	10415			
Building Name/ Address Plaque	10420			
Architect's Plaque	10420			
Roof-Mounted Sign	10430			
Wall-Mounted Sign	10440			

PROTECTIVE COVERS
Cost category: _ A _ B _ C

Covered Walkway	10531
Canopy	10531
Car Shelter	10532
Marquee	10533
Awning	10535

POSTAL SPECIALTIES
Cost category: _ A _ B _ C

| Mail Chute | 10551 |
| Mailbox | 10552 |

SUN-CONTROL
DEVICES
Cost category: _ A _ B _ C

| Sun Screen | 10700 |

TELEPHONE ENCLOSURES
Cost category: _ A _ B _ C

| Telephone Booth | 10750 |

EXTERIOR DESIGN AND CONSTRUCTION (cont.)

DIVISION 11--EQUIPMENT

	Y	M	WHO.WHEN.WHY	NOTES AND REVISIONS

SECURITY AND VAULT
EQUIPMENT
Cost category: _ A _ B _ C

Automatic Teller 11025
Depository
Slot/Box 11026

PARKING EQUIPMENT
Cost category: _ A _ B _ C

Parking Gate 11151
Parking Ticket
Dispenser 11152

LOADING DOCK EQUIPMENT
Cost category: _ A _ B _ C

Loading Dock 11160 _____

Loading Dock
Shelter 11164 _____

WASTE-HANDLING
EQUIPMENT
Cost category: _A_ _B_ _C_

Incinerator 11171 _____
Compactor 11172 _____
Waste Bin 11173 _____
Waste Chute/
Collector 11175 _____

TELECOMMUNICATION
EQUIPMENT
Cost category: _A_ _B_ _C_

Telecommunications
Satellite
Antenna 11800/
16781 _____

221

EXTERNAL DESIGN AND CONSTRUCTION (cont.)

DIVISION 12--FURNISHINGS

		Y	M	WHO.WHEN.WHY	NOTES AND REVISIONS
ARTWORK					
Mural	12110	___	___	___ . ___ . ___	_____
Statuary	12140	___	___	___ . ___ . ___	_____
Bas-Relief	12150	___	___	___ . ___ . ___	_____
Stained Glass	12170	___	___	___ . ___ . ___	_____

DIVISION 13--SPECIAL CONSTRUCTION

SOLAR ENERGY SYSTEMS
Cost category: _A _B _C ___ ___ . ___ _____

Solar Heat
 Collection Panel 13980 ___ ___ . ___ _____
Solar
 Water Heater 13980 ___ ___ . ___ _____

DIVISION 14--CONVEYING SYSTEMS

ELEVATORS

Cost category: _A_ _B_ _C_

	A	B	C
Exterior Elevator 14210			
Hoist 14300			
Crane 14300			

LIFTS

Cost category: _A_ _B_ _C_

	A	B	C
People Lift 14410			
Sidewalk Lift 14411			
Wheelchair Lift 14415			
Vehicle Lift 14450			
Exterior Escalator 14710			
Exterior Moving Walk 14720			

223

EXTERIOR DESIGN AND CONSTRUCTION (cont.)

EXTERIOR DESIGN--ROOF CONSTRUCTION

The following design decisions can and should often be made prior
to the formal design process. For roof framing and slab construction decision checklists, see the section on STRUCTURE.

	Y	M	WHO·WHEN·WHY	NOTES AND REVISIONS

Roof shape

Framing

Slopes

Finish roofing

Flashing type

Overhang

Parapet

EXTERIOR DESIGN AND CONSTRUCTION   (cont.)
EXTERIOR DESIGN--ROOF CONSTRUCTION   (cont.)

	Y	M	WHO·WHEN·WHY	NOTES AND REVISIONS

DIVISION 3--CONCRETE

CONCRETE SLAB/DECK
Cost category: _A _B _C

Rooftop Concrete
  Parking Slab   03300
  Concrete Slab
  Roof Terrace   03300

DIVISION 6--WOOD

ROUGH CARPENTRY
Cost category: _A _B _C

Wood Decking   06125
Duckboard   06125

DIVISION 7--THERMAL AND MOISTURE PROTECTION

SHINGLES AND
ROOFING TILES
Cost category: _A _B

Asphalt				
Shingle Roof	07311			
Wood Shingle/				
Shake Roof	07313			
Slate				
Shingle Roof	07314			
Metal				
Shingle Roof	07316			
Clay Tile Roof	07321			
Concrete				
Tile Roof	07322			

PREFORMED ROOFING
Cost category: _A _B _C

Preformed			
Metal Roof	07412		

EXTERIOR DESIGN AND CONSTRUCTION (cont.)
EXTERIOR DESIGN--ROOF CONSTRUCTION (cont.)

DIVISION 7--THERMAL AND MOISTURE PROTECTION (cont.)

	Y	M	WHO.WHEN.WHY	NOTES AND REVISIONS

MEMBRANE ROOFING
Cost category: _A _B _

Built-Up Roofing 07510
Protected
Membrane Roofing 07550
Reflective
Membrane Roofing 07560

TRAFFIC TOPPING
Cost category: _A _B _C

Traffic Topping 07570
Jogging Track/
Athletic Surface 07570
Decorative
Roof Topping 07570

ROOF ACCESSORIES--
SKYLIGHTS
Cost category: _ A _ B _ C

Skylight	07810			
Skylight Wire				
Mesh Guard	07810			
Plastic Skylight	07811			
Metal-Framed				
Skylight	07812			

DIVISION 8--DOORS AND WINDOWS

SPECIAL WINDOWS
Cost category: _ A _ B _ C

Monitor	08655			

DIVISION 10--SPECIALTIES

FIREPLACES/STOVES
Cost category: _ A _ B _ C

Prefab Chimney	10300/			
	15616			

229

EXTERIOR DESIGN AND CONSTRUCTION (cont.)
EXTERIOR DESIGN--ROOF CONSTRUCTION (cont.)

DIVISION 10--SPECIALTIES (cont.)

	Y	M	WHO.WHEN.WHY	NOTES AND REVISIONS

PREFABRICATED STEEPLES,
SPIRES/CUPOLAS
Cost category: _A _B _C

Steeple 10341
Spire 10342
Cupola 10343

FLAGPOLES 10350
Cost category: _A _B _C

IDENTIFYING DEVICES
Cost category: _A _B _C

Illuminated Sign 10430
Sign 10440
Rooftop Build.
Identification
Marker 10440

PROTECTIVE COVERS
Cost category: _A _B _C

Canopy   10530
Marquee   10530

SUN-CONTROL
DEVICES   10700
Cost category: _A _B _C

DIVISION 11--EQUIPMENT

MAINTENANCE EQUIPMENT
Cost category: _A _B _C

Window-Washing
  Equipment   11012
Window-Washing
  Equipment
  Penthouse   11012
Window-Washing
  Equipment
  Pipe Rail/Gate   11012

231

EXTERIOR DESIGN AND CONSTRUCTION (cont.)
EXTERIOR DESIGN--ROOF CONSTRUCTION (cont.)

DIVISION 13--SPECIAL CONSTRUCTION

	Y	M	WHO·WHEN·WHY	NOTES AND REVISIONS
SPECIAL PURPOSE ROOMS/ BUILDINGS				
Cost category: _A _B _C				
Cooling Tower Enclosure 13130				
Mechanical Room Penthouse 13130				
Stair Bulkhead 13130				
Water Storage Tank Enclosure 13130				
POOLS				
Cost category: _A _B _C				
Rooftop Swimming Pool 13150				

SOLAR ENERGY SYSTEMS
Cost category: _A _B _C

Solar Heat
  Collection Panel 13980
  Water Heater   13980
                   15431
Flat Collector   13981
Solar Concentrating
  Collector   13982
Solar Housing/
  Framing   13985
Packaged Solar
  System   13986

WIND ENERGY
SYSTEMS   13990
Cost category: _A _B _C

DIVISION 15--MECHANICAL

ROOF PLUMBING
Cost category: _A _B _C

Domestic Solar
  Water Heater   15431

233

DIVISION 16--ELECTRICAL

	Y	M	WHO.WHEN.WHY	NOTES AND REVISIONS
LIGHTING Cost category: _ A _ B _ C				
Exterior Building Lighting 16520				
Aircraft Warning Light 16560				
COMMUNICATIONS Cost category: _ A _ B _ C				
TV Tower Master Antenna 16781				
Satellite Dish Antenna 16781 11800				
Broadcast Antenna 16790				

HEATING AND COOLING
Cost category: _ A _ B _ C _

Electric Snow-
Melting Cables   16858   _____

APPURTENANCES

section begins on next page.

235

APPURTENANCES

DIVISION 15--MECHANICAL

	Y	M	WHO.WHEN.WHY	NOTES AND REVISIONS

LIQUID HEAT TRANSFER
Cost category: _ A _ B _ C

Radiant Panel	15745				
Baseboard Unit	15751				
Finned Tube	15752				
Convector	15733				
Radiator	15754				
Unit Heater	15760				
Fan Coil Unit	15761				
Unit Ventilator	15762				
	16850				
Humidifier	15781				

DIVISION 16--ELECTRICAL

LIGHTING
Cost category: _ A _ B _ C

Item	Code	A	B	C
Fluorescent Fixture	16501			
Light Diffuser	16501			
	09120			
Spotlight	16501			
Chandelier	16501			
Surface-Mounted Light Fixture	16510			
Recessed Fixture	16510			
Lighting Track	16510			
Luminous Ceiling	16515			
	09120			
Exterior Building Lighting	16520			
Site Lighting	16530			

SPECIAL SYSTEMS
Cost category: _A_ _B_ _C_

Item	Code	A	B	C
Lightning Protection	16601			
Emergency Light and Power	16610			
Generator	16612			
Cathodic Protection	16640			
Electromagnetic Shielding	16650			

237

APPURTENANCES (cont.)

DIVISION 16--ELECTRICAL (cont.)

COMMUNICATIONS
Cost category: _A _B _C

	Y	M	WHO.WHEN.WHY	NOTES AND REVISIONS
Burglar Detector 16720				
Fire Detector 16721				
Fire Alarm 16721				
Smoke Detector 16725				
Burglar Alarm 16727				
Clock System 16730				
Special Phone System 16740				
Intercom System 16760				
Public Address System 16770				
Annunciator 16770				
Closed Circuit TV Monitor 16780				
Surveillance TV Camera 16780				
TV Tower Master Roof Antenna 16781				

Roof Broad-
casting Antenna 16790 |

ELECTRICAL
HEATING AND COOLING
Cost category: _A _B _C

Electric
  Heating Coils 16860 |
Electric
  Baseboard 16865 |
Packaged Room
  Air Conditioner 16870 |
Radiant Heater 16880 |
Electric Heater 16890 |

239

Index

Note: Page numbers in *italic* indicate illustrations.

About the Author

Fred A. Stitt, architect, is one of the leading writers and researchers in the architecture field today.

His special studies at the University of California at Berkeley's College of Environmental Design focused on advanced computerized methods of architectural planning and led to the publication *Architectural Planning*. Two other manuals, *Creative Problem Solving* and *Breakthroughs in Architectural Practice*, were also based on Fred Stitt's research. He is the author of two popular books for McGraw-Hill, *Systems Drafting* and *Systems Graphics*.

Today, Fred Stitt is the editor of the influential newsletter *Guidelines*, which is read each month by over 6000 design professionals.